"*The Life of the Body* skillfully illustrates how God mediates transforming grace through the God-created body and its senses. Carefully researched and winsomely written, the book offers constructive protocols for formation into Christlikeness and optimal health. Here is an engaging contribution to vital spirituality and physical wellness, or total-person shalom."

Bruce Demarest, senior professor of Christian formation, Denver Seminary, and author of *Seasons of the Soul*

"*The Life of the Body* is a timely gift to the body of Christ, which, even today, stands guilty of the tendency to split off the body from the whole notion of spirituality. The authors' work is richly informative and educational, highly practical and—to my own embarrassment—personally convicting! A much-needed corrective to our misguided understanding of what holistic formation is about."

Wil Hernandez, Andrews Chair in Spiritual Formation at Spring Arbor University and author of *Henri Nouwen and Spiritual Polarities*

"Through the wisdom of their words, through numerous probing questions and through embodied spiritual exercises, Valerie and Lane artfully show us how, in love and obedience, to present our bodies as living sacrifices to our Lord who sacrificed his body for us. In a day when the physical body is used as a tool for selfish pleasure or neglected as excess baggage on a more 'spiritual' journey, *The Life of the Body* provides a sturdy corrective and a refreshing way forward. The hopeful result that the faithful reader can expect, along with the apostle Paul, is that 'Christ will be exalted in my body.'"

Howard Baker, instructor of Christian formation at Denver Seminary and author of *The One T*

"In a gentle, humble, yet firm way, Valerie and Lane have ventured into a subject where few authors have dared to go. I appreciate the way they challenge us as persons with individual bodies and members of Christ's body to examine our issues and embrace the healing offered in Christ."

Richella Parham, ImpartingGrace.com

"Do body wisdom and spiritual formation belong together? Two experienced Christian teachers of spiritual formation say yes. Valerie Hess and Lane Arnold give us an energizing workout for the weary soul, suggesting ways to discard the burden of bad ideas and false behavior in favor of energetic Christ-living that works on many levels. An encouraging book."

Emilie Griffin, author, *Souls in Full Sail* and *Green Leaves for Later Years*

"The risen Christ said, 'Touch me and see.' Valerie Hess and Lane Arnold illuminate the truth that resurrection life is lived in and through our bodies. As the authors reclaim the long-neglected relationships between spirit, mind and body, we discover grace-filled ways to discover life abundant in Christ. I heartily recommend this book."

Karen Wright Marsh, executive director, Theological Horizons

"There are a handful of books that I couldn't stop thinking about after I put them down. *The Life of the Body* is one of them. It is thought-provoking, insightful and well-grounded. . . . If you want to push yourself toward who you are intended to be, let this book challenge your assumptions."

Keith Eigel, cofounder of The Leaders Lyceum

Valerie E. Hess
and Lane M. Arnold

THE LIFE OF THE BODY

Physical Well-Being and Spiritual Formation

IVP Books

An imprint of InterVarsity Press
Downers Grove, Illinois

InterVarsity Press
P.O. Box 1400, Downers Grove, IL 60515-1426
World Wide Web: www.ivpress.com
E-mail: email@ivpress.com

InterVarsity Press® is the book-publishing division of InterVarsity Christian Fellowship/USA®, a movement of students and faculty active on campus at hundreds of universities, colleges and schools of nursing in the United States of America, and a member movement of the International Fellowship of Evangelical Students. For information about local and regional activities, write Public Relations Dept., InterVarsity Christian Fellowship/USA, 6400 Schroeder Rd., P.O. Box 7895, Madison, WI 53707-7895, or visit the IVCF website at <www.intervarsity.org>.

Scripture quotations, unless otherwise noted, are from the New Revised Standard Version of the Bible, copyright 1989 by the Division of Christian Education of the National Council of the Churches of Christ in the USA. Used by permission. All rights reserved.

While all stories in this book are true, some names and identifying information in this book have been changed to protect the privacy of the individuals involved.

Cover design: Cindy Kiple
Interior design: Beth Hagenberg
Images: A woman on beach: © Fred Froese/iStockphoto
      orange slice: © Dimitris Stephanides/iStockphoto

ISBN 978-0-8308-3571-3

Printed in the United States of America ∞

Library of Congress Cataloging-in-Publication Data has been requested.

P	18	17	16	15	14	13	12	11	10	9	8	7	6	5	4	3	2	1
Y	27	26	25	24	23	22	21	20	19	18	17	16	15	14	13	12		

Valerie's Dedication
For John, Maggie and Lydia:
God's great gifts and the source of
much of what is good in my life.

Lane's Dedication
To the joys of my heart who journey
with me to the wild, inviting heart
of Jesus, the One ever for us,
bringing new freedoms:

Beloved Robert,
without whom second chances would be just
an old country love song, instead of
a daily serenade of joy

Susannah,
whose sass and risk-taking encourage my own

Nathan,
whose tales bring long laughter and longer talks

Jeremy,
whose steadfast heart steadies my own

Christina,
who is ever expectant with hope and good cheer

Jonathan,
who starts the wonder of a new generation

Contents

Introduction

Here's the Question

I (Valerie) teach a practicum in the spiritual disciplines for the
Master of Arts in Spiritual Formation and Leadership (MSFL)
program at Spring Arbor University. I require students to choose a
way to discipline their bodies along with learning new tools to
discipline their minds, emotions and spirits. This assignment
springs from the idea that the definition of "wholeness" includes
being fully integrated as a human being, body, mind and spirit;
therefore, physical health and spiritual formation are closely related. Wanting to more fully explore the question "Is the physical
body and its health relevant to spiritual formation, and if so, how?"
I chose to test that theory on a wider group by making a bodily
discipline a requirement of the class.

Some students find this a curious requirement. What could exercise, resting more or losing some weight have to do with the
loftier goal of being conformed to the likeness of Christ? What
do our bodies have to do with spiritual formation? In the course,
students choose bodily disciplines, such as adding in exercise,
giving up some onerous eating habit, like sugar or soda pop, or
committing to more sleep each week.

After teaching several rounds of the course, a real connection became clear. My students and I noticed the relationship between what was happening in our bodies and what was happening in our souls. The most obvious connection came for all of us during the discipline of fasting unit, but surprisingly, it also started to make sense within other spiritual discipline practices such as prayer, worship and Bible study. In final papers, students often reflected on the connections between what they were doing to discipline their body and how they were seeking to discipline other aspects of their life. One student shared this in the final paper:

> Why a bodily discipline? How does this help my spiritual formation and the practice of the spiritual disciplines? When I take care of my body, with good food and an active lifestyle, I can tell the difference in other parts of my life. When I am more mentally alert, more joyful, and well rested, I can see the difference in so many other areas of my life. While I am reading a book, working on homework, or doing one of my many crazy job responsibilities, I feel more up to the task. This feeling of joy and productivity only increases when I combine this bodily discipline with the spiritual disciplines. The combination of the two allows me to take on the world with a new kind of enthusiasm.[1]

Where in life have you noticed an intersection between how your body feels and how your spirit responds to God?

CONNECTING THE DOTS BETWEEN BODY AND SOUL

I (Lane) came to this topic from a different perspective, over the course of a lifetime. I grew up in the South, surrounded by comfort foods galore. Every meal contained sweets: sweet rolls or coffee cake for breakfast, cookies and ice cream at lunch, and some kind of delicious cake, cobbler or other confectionary for dessert at dinner. Sweet tea and cola were the beverages most likely served at any given meal. Unsurprisingly, I have a sweet tooth. If it wasn't sweet, it was usually fried or lightly breaded. Biscuits, cornbread and rolls topped with butter, jam, jelly or gravy were standard fare in the South when I grew up. Exercise for girls, however, was not standard fare.

Being a home economics major with a child development concentration, college work focused on how children developed, as well as nutrition and body care during prenatal, infant and childhood years. During one semester, when living in the home economics house as required, we integrated our daily life and daily learning. Budgeting, healthy eating, purchasing foods from the perimeter of the grocery store and meals together demonstrated integration of our book learning. A subtle shift began in what I ate and how I exercised.

My exploration of food and exercise continued while caring for my body during pregnancy and childbirth, then raising three children. Like most young seminary students' families, the budget created the bottom line. I aimed for creating healthy baby food, alternative sweet treats, and meals that were nutritious and delicious, made from scratch. As you can imagine, however, with three children under three-and-a-half years old, some days I was just thankful to get any semblance of a meal on the table. Exercise, however, was woven into the fabric of life. Someone was always in motion, and so was I. Looking back, I see that it was rare to consider that what I ate or fed others or what happened in my body might somehow correlate with my heart's relationship with Jesus.

After twenty years of marriage, profound loss in the form of divorce left a sour taste. The toll was not just on my heart or on my emotions, but also on my body. The raggedness of my heart showed up in frazzled ways, affecting my sleep, teeth, energy and weight.

Raising three marvelous teenagers full time on my own while being an elementary school teacher stretched me every which way. Exercise and food became a jumble in the midst of just surviving each day. Being unaware of the impact that stress, grief, frustration and other assorted emotions can have, I didn't really connect the dots between what my heart was saying to my body or what my body was saying to my heart.

All the while, a sweetness of another kind was developing, a deeper-than-ever intimacy with Jesus. In the stress and loneliness that ensued after divorce, Jesus came as a Lover, wooing me to joy. One day, in talking with Jesus, I wondered if I'd ever again have any reason to create a romantic meal for anyone, one full of love and beauty. Jesus gently persuaded me to shift my thinking. Why not create every meal as an act of love and beauty, a way of showing my love for my forever Lover? From there forward, my heart shifted. Times of fun and fellowship with family and friends were always laced with simple touches that one sweetheart might do for another. It no longer mattered that I didn't have a physical sweetheart; I delighted in being the Beloved of Christ and, in turn, offered that love to others. Meals became life-giving delights, times of joy savored with my own teenagers and their friends alongside other single and married friends of mine. Rather than entertaining to impress, hospitality invited others to know the wonder of a heart being restored by my Lover Jesus.

As my children finished up college, transitioning to grad school or new careers, I mirrored their youthful enthusiasms. Retired by then from teaching elementary school, I returned to Colorado, a place I had once called home, and entered seminary, a new adventure for my healing heart. Yet, unexpectedly, my delightful single life took another turn. Aging parents suddenly required my full-time care back in Georgia. Not versed in geriatrics, I garnered medical, nutritional and exercise information on the mental and physical needs of my mother and dad, while also aiming to eat wisely and exercise when I could. I knew that if I didn't take good care of my own health, I would be fairly worthless as a caregiver for two 80-plus-year-olds. The relationship between my body and my heart began to emerge in fresh ways. When I was wise in caring for both my body and my heart, I was more attuned to Christ, thus better able to offer care for my parents. The converse was also true.

Back in seminary in Colorado after those caregiving times, I started connecting the dots. Reading Christian classics and contemporary journals on soul care, spiritual formation, spiritual disciplines and spiritual direction, pictures began to form. Entering into a spiritual direction relationship as a directee, I noticed the ways my body influenced my heart. Being a spiritual director for others, the same similarities began to surface within my own directees. The body speaks to the heart. The heart speaks to the body. All of this connects deeply to the heart of Jesus. Would I pay attention to those connections?

Some of my directees, though, were resistant to pondering such a connection. They uncomfortably felt that perhaps this body-heart connection was somehow associated with "New Age" thought. "Is it really Christ-centered to notice one's body, rather than just one's heart?" a directee would ask. "Places of resistance are worth taking note of, aren't they?" would be my response.

A plethora of questions popped up for my directees, and for me as well. What did wisdom look like when it came to caring for my body through exercise and nutrition? What was clean eating? What did a holy rhythm of life for body and heart look like? Did any of this have anything to do with intimacy with Christ? Did inner healing of emotions and wounds from my past translate to exterior healing and bodily care?

Desiring an integrated body and heart, new crossroads appeared for pondering, as Jeremiah 6:16 states. I discovered surprising places of resistance to the good ways, because the comfortable ways were easier, and much more familiar. What might move me forward from my stuck places? For me, the prayer of examen led to a more courageously examined, intentional life of both body and heart.

Another unexpected season arrived, one of great joy. My high school and college sweetheart found me. After a thirty-four-year absence of communication, God gave us back to one another. Four years ago, we married and merged two hearts and two bodies who approached fitness and food with entirely differing perspectives. Shortly thereafter I began the Spiritual Exercises of St. Ignatius, where I noticed the interplay of body and heart in new ways. Within the Ignatian Exercises, the retreatant journeys through the life of Christ, while noticing how God is present in one's own life. Watching Jesus, I also watched myself. Noticing Christ, I noticed changes in both the exterior and interior places of my life. Changes brought questions; questions brought changes.

So, here I am, a long way from all the comfort foods of the South, finding delicious comfort in seeing how God invites me to connect my heart and my body, how Christ feeds me with food for my heart that nourishes both body and soul. Do I still have disconnects between my heart and my body, between the words I say and the life I live? Of course. I struggle with being consistent about eating wisely and exercising regularly. My body is not where I'd like it to be. It is soft where I'd like it to be firm, and firmly entrenched where I'd love to see more fluidity. But, so is my heart. I'd like to tell you that I have it all figured out. I'd like to tell you that I write to tell you all the answers about the body-heart connection. But if you took one glance at my body and took the time to know my heart, you'd know that is not the case. I am in process toward integrating body and heart into whole and holy living with Jesus, by connecting the dots to form a picture of wholeness and holiness. All that Jesus is involves all that I am, body, heart, soul, spirit and mind.

WHAT ABOUT YOU?

How aware are you of this connection between what happens to your body and what happens to your soul? Is your morning "quiet time" different when you are not feeling well than when you are rested and feeling strong? Similarly, when struggling with a problem or having a "dark" day, have you noticed a feeling of "weightiness" in your body that is not there when you are happy? Perhaps you even slouch a bit on those kinds of days.

Since God created us to be whole, integrated beings, spiritual formation happens in all seasons of life, for good or for ill. The training or discipline in one part of our life is directly affected by the training, or lack thereof, going on in another part of our life. For example, engaging in a weight-loss program with a large component of public accountability, I (Valerie) also had success in changing other areas of my life, such as negative thoughts and spending habits. Discipline in one area of life can carry over into other areas of life in significant ways, easily crossing between that which impacts the body and that which impacts the soul.

Our physical bodies play an important role in following Christ. However, we are not always aware of that fact. Plato heavily influences Western Christians. He taught that the body and soul are irreconcilable enemies. Plato conceded that we need a body to carry the soul around but believed the body to be a lower entity than the soul. He taught that our energies are best directed to matters of the soul alone and that the things of the material world are not worth bothering with.

That, however, is not the message of the Bible, which integrates body and soul in a whole and holy way. The Bible says that the body is the temple of the Holy Spirit and promises that it will be raised at Jesus' second coming. Likewise, the earth and all of creation will be part of that final resurrection at the last day.[2] God's pronouncement of creation as "good" in Genesis 1–2 has not been rescinded; neither has the charge to humanity to be a steward of that creation. The material world, though fallen, is still redeemable. Otherwise, Jesus would not have been born a man, died on the cross and then been resurrected with a new body that could eat fish.

Because of Jesus, the stewardship of our bodies and the care of creation have a "spiritual formation" side to them. Is exercising equally as important as Bible reading? If time is limited, isn't it a better choice to have prayer time and neglect the exercise? Scripture actually invites us to embrace both. Plato's insidious, subtle and pervasive notion may be why many of us have never considered the close connection between physical health and spiritual formation.

"Preach the gospel at all times, and when necessary, use words." These words attributed to St. Francis of Assisi sum up one theme of this book: our physical presence may compel people toward or away from Christ. With our physical bodies, we bear a message of what we believe about God, the world and ourselves. Additionally, the material world is a witness to God (Psalm 19) and is worthy of care. Creation in all of its vast diversity awaits the redemption of humanity, its pinnacle (Romans 8:19-23). Just as St. Francis called the sun "brother" and the moon "sister," so Christ-followers also show the world the real

How do you currently preach the gospel without using words?

reason for living in environmentally friendly ways. We live as children of God, the Creator of the universe, loving and caring for the world in ways similar to how God does.

WHY WE WROTE THE BOOK

The two of us have been mulling over these body and heart connections for some time. This book is our attempt to strengthen the connection between the two parts that comprise human beings: the physical and the spiritual. These two entities are not ultimately divisible from each other, though some try to sever that connection. In profound ways, the unity of the body with the soul influences our walk with Christ, a concept that can be difficult to grasp at times. It is often an uncomfortable "elephant in the room": something people don't want to speak of yet strongly suspect is very important. Perhaps you, too, have had this experience: someone in your circle of friends asks regularly for prayers of physical healing, yet they continue to indulge in poor health habits, which contribute significantly to their disease/dis-ease. How do we speak in love toward those people about their choices? Should we even bring up the choices and habits? Was Plato correct when he taught that the body is less important than one's soul? These are unsettling issues to wrestle with, aren't they? We believe these issues are worth bringing to the table for honest reflection and open discussion.

The two of us became acquainted through Renovaré conferences and mutual friends. We found ourselves discussing the impact of the physical body and its health on a person's spiritual formation, comparing notes about the subject. Appropriately, while lunching at a local café, the idea of a shared writing project began. Sometimes the book you write is the one you couldn't find to read. Though there certainly are a plethora of books with tidbits here and chapters there about the physical body and its relation to the interior life, we couldn't find one that addressed the variety of issues we were mulling over. Conversations led to inquisitive chapters, a natural progression for people like the two of us who process best while writing. We soon realized that each topic could easily be a book in itself. Our goal with this book is to introduce the issues and questions surrounding the topic of the body, the heart and our life with Christ, trusting that readers will pursue further topics that interest them.

A word of caution: the two of us do not always agree on what the issues, or the questions within those issues, are. Our readers will also find plenty of places to diverge from our ideas. That is to be expected; we want to begin a lively discussion within broad circles about these topics.

Also, know that we are not nutritionists, although we both enjoy eating and cooking nutritional meals. Neither of us is a personal trainer, gym teacher, coach or professional athlete, though both of us enjoy being outside and active. Neither of us has a perfect body, though both of us are perfectly thankful for the body we inhabit each day. Both of us struggle with issues involving physical health and spiritual formation, even as we are more convinced than ever that the intersection of the two is important.

This book is the result of our ponderings. It is our attempt to look at issues that surround the question "Is the physical body and its health related to spiritual formation?" We will share some ideas of how each person might choose to answer that. We will look at what it means to be a wise steward of the body in a culture where obesity rates, due to junk food and lack of exercise, are epidemic. We will talk about extreme body worship as evidenced in popular culture. We invite you to join us in discovering areas of life where the notion of preaching the gospel without using words is lived out.

BODY ISSUES WITHIN THE BODY

Often defensiveness and discomfort surround this subject of the life of the body. Deformity or chronic illnesses are mentioned as reasons why it is "wrong" or "inappropriate" to ask if the body has anything to do with one's spiritual formation. Faced with a Christ-follower who is struggling with a physical challenge of some kind, we often feel we have no right to say anything to them about choices they are making. We struggle to discern where the line is between offending someone and speaking truth in love. This is difficult to do at times. Yet, even deformity or chronic illnesses must be looked at in terms of how those hardships impact a person's spiritual formation. And within chronic physical challenges, there are still choices to be made daily that strengthen what health we have or diminish it.

Poor lifestyle choices that lead to illness are another category. These, too, call for special care and sensitivity. How do we walk with those who have diabetes or heart disease, which came about as a result of a lifetime of poor eating habits and/or little to no exercise? How can we bear with another's affliction in love while encouraging a change in habits?

Suffering, until recently, was an assumed part of a life of faith for Christ's followers. Today, we do all we can to ensure that we do not have to suffer. Does this spring from the subtle heresy that the disciples also struggled with: if you are blessed with health and wealth, God loves you more (Mark 10:23-27)? How can the larger body of Christ help us wisely care for our individual bodies in God-pleasing ways? Or should it?

Plato's ideas separate the "lower" material world from the "higher" realities of the soul. When we live with that idea, consciously or un-

What do you believe the role of suffering is in the life of a Christ-follower?

consciously, we shift from God's view. The Bible views the body and soul as an integrated whole. Jesus modeled wholeness and holiness when he came to earth as a human being. Plato's notion, however, allows us to more easily buy the lie that "my body is my own," instead of seeing it as a gift from God. While our bodies are the vehicles through which our souls interact with the world, Scripture tells us that they are also the temple of the Holy Spirit. Yet, many of us function out of the belief that what we do to our bodies really doesn't matter, as these bodies will be discarded at death. We live as if we haven't fully understood that our bodies will also be resurrected at Jesus' second coming.

Perhaps we, as members of the body of Christ, have done ourselves a disservice here. Without a godly view of the material world, we lack the language and tools to integrate our physical bodies as part of our spiritual formation. By talking about a person's soul to the exclusion of their physical being, we dishonor the wholeness of the individual bodies of Christ that make up the corporate body of Christ. We hope people will begin to reconnect their body's welfare to the heart's, and vice versa. Our passion is to introduce a more integrated view of wholeness and holiness of the life of the body within the body of Christ.

HOW TO USE THIS BOOK

At the end of each chapter, there are three exercises provided for the reader to actively experience some of the chapter's concepts. They are an important part of the core message of this book. Change occurs through actively engaging with an idea, not just reading about it. Though you may be tempted to skip over them, experiencing some of these exercises will give you a deeper grasp of the concepts in each chapter. In addition, feel free to create your own exercises if the ones suggested simply do not engage you right now.

Appendix A looks at holy habits, the spiritual disciplines, from a physical perspective. Appendix B provides Scripture passages that refer to the physical body. Appendix C offers additional resources for more fully exploring the chapters' themes. Appendix D is the small group guide. Using these appendices, individuals and small groups can delve deeper into the book's topics.

May this volume help all of us preach the good news of Jesus Christ more fully, with or without words.

CLOSING PRAYER

Lord, I confess I don't connect the dots often enough about the idea that what goes on with my body affects what goes on with my heart and soul. My body hasn't always seemed all that important to my Christian growth. But here, in this reading of this book, I'd like to reconsider my body and how it relates to your body, the church.

Would you keep me attentive? I ask that I might be mindful of my body, to notice that just as the stars in the heavens, the flowers of the fields and the birds of the air show me something of you, so does my body, which you made.

I admit that it would be easier to ignore the flaws and struggles of this body I live in, or to stay focused only on the flaws and struggles. It would be easier to just wait to trade it in for a new model, one that is redeemed after I leave earth, but I suppose ease isn't all that it's cracked up to be. Besides, I am noticing that sometimes this body, which is my vehicle for travel here on earth, needs a bit of renovation, just as my heart does each day.

So, I come to you, Jesus. I ponder your body. I ponder mine. I ponder what you are up to in the invitation of this book's premise: a body that matters to the ways my spiritual formation occurs. You call me your Bride, your Beloved. May I see the beauty in me that is there because of your invitation to life: body, heart, soul, mind and spirit. Amen.

REFLECTION EXERCISES

1. In Valerie's practicum class on the spiritual disciplines, students chose a body discipline as one way of seeking to integrate their interior and exterior life. What, if any, bodily health disciplines are you currently engaged in? Are there any you are avoiding? Is there one you might consider trying out today, and for the next week? Why or why not?

2. What do you think of your body? Is it a source of joy or a burden? Do you feel completely detached from the physical world or like an integral part of the physical world? Spend some time journaling about where you stand on the continuum. Ask God to show you areas where you need healing concerning images you have of your body, maybe even forgiving those who instilled those negative images in you.

3. Explore what you think God says about the human body. Here are a few Scripture passages to start with: Genesis 1–2; Psalm 139; Luke 11:33-36; 1 Corinthians 6:12-20 and 1 Peter 4:1-6. Appendix B lists some more. Take some time to reflect on your body. Where did those beliefs about your body originate? Did you inherit them from your family of origin, the media around you, your peers or from those that are recorded in Scripture?

1

Jesus Has a Body

Jesus came to earth as a human being through Mary's womb. That event affirms us in our own bodies. He ate. He slept. He walked. He laughed. He cried. He touched. The concrete reality of the Incarnation is its uniqueness: God as a person, here in a body, like us, on a physical earth, with us.

Yet, as Christ-followers, we believe that Jesus continues to have a body, a mystery that says Jesus is fully God and fully human, body and soul. That mystery continues as we confess his body being resurrected and then ascended into heaven. Jesus is alive today and has a body, though different from the one he had on earth, as ours will be someday. In this chapter, though, we will be focusing on Jesus' earthly body.

Immanuel, God-with-us, is the historical reality of God among us, not just in spirit but also in the physicalness of an earthly body. This Incarnation, where Jesus the fully divine God lived for a while among us in his physical body as fully man, is both a vital Christian doctrine and a wondrous reality. While it is true that the Incarnation has profound theological implications, it also has pragmatic implications for how we live our life in a physical body. For thirty-three years Jesus offered a physical glimpse of the spiritual life with

God, modeling for us how to live a fully integrated exterior and interior life.

God thought enough of the human body to send Jesus forth in bodily form. Watch how Jesus treated his own body while also encouraging the disciples and others that he encountered over those earthly years. We begin to see the immense value God has for the physical body as we behold Jesus. Psalm 139:13-14 reminds us:

> For it was you who formed my inward parts;
> you knit me together in my mother's womb.
> I praise you, for I am fearfully and wonderfully made.
> Wonderful are your works;
> that I know very well.

Fearfully and wonderfully made. That's what the God who created us has to say about us. This body we inhabit is fearfully and wonderfully made, yet we don't fully live as if that were true. Fearfully and wonderfully made, yet often this body is viewed as not all that important to the formation of my heart and my life with God.

We choose our attitude and perspective about our body based on our theology, our culture, our past upbringing and our emotions of the moment. Three basic attitudes exist: we are contented and connected to our body as a holy dwelling place of the Living God; we dismiss our body as irrelevant to our walk with God; we revere our body at the expense of our worship of God. Because we often do not have a sound theology of what our body is to God, how we are to treat our body, and what our body has to do with our spiritual life and growth, we are often tempted to simply dismiss our body as not all that important, at least as compared to spiritual things.

The reality is that we are given a body by God, our Creator, to inhabit for the years we live on this earth. This body is indeed fearfully and wonderfully made by our God who quite unashamedly adores each of us, from the top of our head to the bottom of our feet. So, if God so loves us, including our very physical body which he deemed important enough to create, perhaps our perspective, like a pair of old glasses, needs a readjustment of vision.

JESUS IS OUR MODEL

Perhaps it is in looking at Jesus and his relationship to us with his own physical body that we can clarify our vision of this life in the body. The whole of the Incarnation occurred within the framework of a physical body integrated in whole and holy manners with Christ's spiritual life. He did not just appear as a disembodied spirit, though he could have. He didn't float through the years with super-human powers, though he could have. He didn't show up fully grown up, though he could have. Part of the full surrender of Christ in coming to live among us on earth involved becoming fully human, fully of a physical body, just as we are.

Like other people, Jesus grew from infant to toddler to boy to teenager to man. He lived and breathed as we do. When he died, just as we will one day, his body ceased to live and breathe. The difference, of course, is that after three days, he came to life again, resurrected in a physical body. As with Jesus' body, our bodies will be resurrected from the dead. That alone, aside from the vast theological impact, says something about the body. Something that is going to be redeemed is worth caring for; something that is going to be discarded at death isn't worth bothering with.

Too often, we emphasize the death of the body and the ongoing life of the heart, to the point that we forget this fact: in the final resurrection, our body will be raised up and reunited with our heart in a new form. God raised Jesus with a body that could be seen and touched. While the early disciples at times feared he was a ghost, Jesus ate fish and let them touch his nail scars to show them that his body was real. Jesus' resurrection shows us what will happen to us after our death. It is a mystery, but we can await new bodies for ourselves. Our attention to physical health here and now is a statement that we believe in that coming redemption.

A SILENT WITNESS

One way to worship God without ceasing is to live the life God created you to live, as Jesus did. Each of us can be a witness to God's love and goodness by living joyfully and creatively. We seek to be healthy and full of life because our Savior was. Being as healthy and joyful as possible, as individuals as well as the members of the larger body of Christ, we are powerful testimonies: physically, relationally, spiritually, creatively, emotionally and mentally. Physical life supports our spiritual formation that in turn nurtures our physicality.

What would the "best possible version" of yourself look like?

Even though Jesus was also God during his time on earth as a man, there are many life circumstances he never experienced. Jesus, as a human male, could not experience everything that can possibly happen in life, like menopause, labor contractions or losing a limb in combat. He didn't struggle to live with integrity in vast wealth or drive a car. He didn't watch TV or have to respond to emails for his job. Still, Jesus, as a man, showed us how to live our lives now by living one human life well in a specific place in time and history. He gave us a universal template, based on love and service. The way he treated others is a model for us. His taking a break from earthly needs to spend time in prayer gives us permission to do the same. His life had balance, brought into being by the rhythms of rest and work, prayer and playfulness, solitude and togetherness. His desire to be a healing presence in all circumstances is something we can share.

After he ascended back to heaven, he sent his Spirit so that his body on earth, the church, might fill out all the other possible ways of living. We, as that body of Christ, show the world how to live by following the path Jesus walked. For example, we choose joy in all our circumstances, often in spite of our circumstances. We learn to forgive and serve others through Christ's power. We do our daily tasks listening for the voice of our good Shepherd.

At times, we may become discouraged knowing that imitating Christ is impossible because it means living a life like his. But when we live our own life, knowing God loves us, seeking to employ the principles that Jesus taught to our unique circumstances, we are living the Christ-life. We do that in the mundane chores of life as well as in the areas of calling and giftedness that are uniquely ours.

BECOMING ACCESSIBLE

In trying to understand the idea of the Incarnation, God becoming human, I (Valerie) thought of our cat, Butterscotch. He was a lap cat par excellence who lived to be nearly twenty years old. He was very attached to our family, to the point that whenever he saw suitcases coming out, he would go under a chair and "look depressed." Sometimes, if only one of us was leaving, I would look with great empathy at this forlorn animal. I wished with all my heart that I

Have you ever desperately wanted to communicate something to someone but weren't able to do so? Maybe you were on a trip in a foreign country. What did you do to try to be understood?

could talk to him in a way he could understand. I wanted to tell him, in his language, that the rest of the family would be home soon. If the whole family was leaving, I wanted him to know that we were not abandoning him. We would come back and, in the meantime, he would be well cared for by the cat sitter.

This is what God did in sending Jesus. By being born as a human baby, Jesus showed us God in a form we could understand more easily. It would be as if I had become a cat, so I could tell Butterscotch about our vacation plans, assuring him that everything would be all right for him too. God in Jesus became one of us so that he could assure us that everything is indeed well, now and forever.

At times, the God of the exodus seemed remote and "other" to the people of Israel. God talked to Moses, telling him how Israel was to live as a holy nation set apart for God's glory. There, in that wilderness encounter, the whole idea of a "mediator" was born, someone who would be the go-between with God and humanity. In the temple in Jerusalem at the time of Christ, no one could go into the Holy of Holies except the High Priest, and then only once a year under strict conditions. God seemed highly inaccessible. However, by Jesus coming in a real body that one could see and hear, God became more accessible to us. God was still holy and above all, but now there was the opportunity to know the face of the Father: it looked like Jesus, who became our mediator (1 Timothy 2:5).

SO WHAT DOES THIS ALL MEAN?

Jesus' coming in the flesh invites us to find ways to "enflesh" ourselves in other's circumstances. Edith Schaeffer, wife of the late Francis Schaeffer and cofounder of the L'Abri community, tells of her parents, missionaries to China. Edith spent some of her childhood in China before the family was forced to leave by the Communists. Edith's father, desiring to be a real part of life in China, not only wore the dress customary to Chinese men of that period, but he grew a real braid.

Do you know someone who went to great lengths to bring the gospel to others? What did they do?

Unlike some missionaries who wore a fake hair braid, Edith's father, so eager to reach the Chinese with the good news of Jesus Christ, became as Chinese as he possibly could. The local people were aware that he let his hair grow long, shaving the front of his head and braiding the pigtail that hung down his back. His seeking to fully identify with their culture made them more open to the words of his mouth. In a similar fashion, St. Paul, in 1 Corinthians 9:19-23, shared with that congregation that he tried to "become all things to all people" so that in some way he might reach some with the good news of Jesus Christ. Paul was modeling his desire to be all things to all people after Jesus, who became one of us to save us. Like Paul, we are invited to "incarnate" the love of God as an offering to those around us.

WHY IT IS IMPORTANT

The doctrine of the Incarnation, the formal phrase the church uses to refer to Jesus' becoming a human being, is not dry or archaic insider jargon. It is a living reality that affects our daily lives. If God so loved the world that he sent his only Son (see John 3:16), then we are to love this world in the same way, starting with our bodies. We are to care for ourselves so that we can care for others.

Some people feel that caring for themselves is self-indulgent. While there is certainly a point where self-care can become self-indulgence, there is also a point where self-neglect inhibits our ability to do the work of the kingdom of God. Exhaustion due to chronic lack of sleep or poor nutrition will lead to ineffective listening to those in need. Health problems due to lack of exercise or the abuse of tobacco, alcohol and drugs will keep us from being able to minister to those around us. Even Jesus walked away from people to spend restorative time in prayer with his Father (see Mark 1:35-38, for example).

Jesus has a body so that he can show us how to live more fully integrated in body and heart within our own body. God could have destroyed everything and started over after the Fall (Genesis 3). Instead, Jesus came to earth, blessing the material world and our bodies with his presence. That is good news, isn't it? May we, echoing Jesus, use these gifts of our body and our heart to further the kingdom of heaven here on earth, as Christ did.

CLOSING PRAYER

Jesus, I ponder your life here on earth. You let go of heaven and took on an earthly body. I must admit that I don't tend to think of you with a stomach that grumbled for its next meal. I've never even thought of how your legs probably ached after walking from town to town. You undoubtedly took time to wash the dust from your face. How odd that must have been. You who created the stream and the sea were dipping your bronzed hands into the coolness to wash your face of dust and dirt, which you also created.

Life of the World, you became human so I could become godly. You understand tiredness and full days. You understand my human need for daily food, and you are far less surprised than I am about the human emotions often attached to food. You know that a walk at dawn invigorates, just as a talk with friends on the road enlivens the journey. You know I need a rhythm of quiet among the rush of the days, as you modeled when you pulled away from the crowd to be alone with your Father.

Lord, sometimes I catch a whiff of heaven. There is this deep longing that brings me to tears, and it is hard to capture in words. But when it happens, I know beyond knowing, deep in my heart, that you have offered me the scent of heaven. It is a moment of Spirit-infused wonder, so deep that it takes my breath away and impacts my physical body. There is an exquisiteness to the longing, to the beauty, to the moment, that is indescribable in mere words.

Sometimes, when that happens, I pause and ponder what leaving heaven must have been like for you. In my life, I have had my share of goodbyes. I have said goodbye to people I have loved, and though I know I'll see them again in a few months or even just a few weeks, my emotions well up. Something deep tugs at me. I have said goodbyes to folks as they have died. That's a tough goodbye, especially because I am so concrete. I love the touch and the words of another, and when they die, I lose that connection. It is even tougher when I do not have any assurance that the person loved you and walked with you, for then, I don't know if I will ever see them again. Knowing you alone is eternal life.

I have said my goodbyes to seasons of life and have found a longing to return to a previous simpler season. I have said my goodbyes to places as well, knowing that I will never return to a particular geographic place or, if I do, that both it and I will have changed.

You know, of course, that I have said some goodbyes adding a muttered "good riddance," huffing in frustration as I said it. Regardless, goodbyes shift something deep within me.

Jesus, what was it like for you to let go of such wonder, such perfection, such fellowship with the Father and the Spirit, to humble yourself and become one of us? How did it tug at your heartstrings to say goodbye? Yet in your goodbye you generously and lavishly offered me the chance to say hello to life, to say hello to forever.

I tend to think of the cross as *the* sacrifice that you made, which, of course, is true. But you gave up the scent of heaven, the scent of home, to come and offer heaven and home for my heart eternally.

Let me not take so lightly the goodbye you said to allow the hello of love to always echo in my heart. Amen.

REFLECTION EXERCISES

1. Many Christmas carols talk about Jesus' birth. For example, in the carol "Hark the Herald Angels Sing" by Charles Wesley, the original second stanza read:

   > Late in time, behold Him come, Offspring of a virgin's womb.
   > Veiled in flesh the Godhead see; Hail the incarnate Deity,
   > Pleased with us in flesh to dwell, Jesus our Emmanuel.
   > Hark the herald angels sing, Glory to the newborn King.

   Spend some time journaling about each phrase of this verse. What are the implications of these words for your daily life? Do an Internet search for the words to other Christmas carols.

What do they say about life in Christ throughout the whole year, not just at Christmastime?

2. Study this section of a very early Christian creed attributed to Athanasius (b. ca. 296-298–d. 2 May 373) called the Athanasian Creed.

> It is necessary for eternal salvation that one also faithfully believe that our Lord Jesus Christ became flesh.
>
> For this is the true faith that we believe and confess: That our Lord Jesus Christ, God's Son, is both God and man.
>
> He is God, begotten before all worlds from the being of the Father, and he is man, born in the world from the being of his mother—existing fully as God, and fully as man with a rational soul and a human body; equal to the Father in divinity, subordinate to the Father in humanity.
>
> Although he is God and man, he is not divided, but is one Christ.
>
> He is united because God has taken humanity into himself; he does not transform deity into humanity.
>
> He is completely one in the unity of his person, without confusing his natures.
>
> For as the rational soul and body are one person, so the one Christ is God and man.

Who is this Jesus and what do we learn of him? What does it tell you about who you are? Meditate on these words for several days.

3. As we reflect on the Incarnation of Jesus, the discipline of worship invites us to praise. Choose to worship Jesus for an hour by yourself this week. Delight in Jesus, fully human, a physical person who came to earth. Delve into devotion over Jesus, fully God. Use these passages as you worship Jesus, Immanuel, God with us: Hebrews 1:1-9; Romans 1:3-4; Philippians 2:5-11; Revelation 19:11-16.

2

Bodies Within the Body

During college, fresh to life with Jesus and enjoying fellowship with other Christ-followers, the words of Acts 2 intrigued me. What if I (Lane) really lived as if all that I was and all that I had was part of something bigger than just me? Canyon-deep conversations developed with seven other students also intrigued by this concept. Kingdom-living dialogues moved from words to actions. We bought, gutted and began renovation on a condemned house in the inner city of Atlanta, Georgia. It was anything but well received by our suburban parents. Our philosophy friends offered quizzical looks: were we of a socialistic mindset? Other Christian acquaintances could not wrap their minds around the fact that men and women could dwell together in that day and age of the sexual revolution without being sexually active with one another. To most, we were an enigma. Moving together through each day within Christian community, attempting to live out Acts 2:42, was, for us, energizing. To this day, almost forty years later, all eight of us think of that time as foundational to our newfound life in Christ as we stretched to live out our faith.

We were one of a number of faith communities that sprang up along the East Coast, inspired by Francis and Edith Schaeffer, who birthed L'Abri, an evangelical fellowship combining study, work and daily life together. L'Abri offered the body of Christ a place of study in a time of doubt. Like many other Christ-centered communities of the 1970s, these holy gatherings contrasted with the popular hippie, free-sex and drug-oriented communes of the time. Basilea, our community, engaged the whole of who we each were: body, heart, soul, mind and spirit. Whether involved in Bible study, prayer, accountability, neighborhood engagement or cooking in the kitchen, living intentionally and intensely together caused us to journey differently than when we just met weekly for Bible study or on weekends for pizza and beer. Unsurprisingly, life together was messy and miserable at times, glorious and gleeful at others, as is typical of family life.

It is far easier to rejoice in one another's triumphs when we don't have to live through the troughs that are trudged in the process. But as we did life together, we moved from a place of head faith to actually being the body of Christ. Doing so involved our physical bodies that we walked around in each day. We ate together and exercised together. We shared a drafty house with unreliable heat. We cared for one another when we were sick, even when we at times were sick of one another. Within a year, our band of believers disbanded to go separate ways: grad school, med school or toward marriage. Individually, we were never the same, having been part of something larger than our small lives.

PART OF ONE ANOTHER

Acts 2 shows how early church believers held everything in common. They shared worship and food. They shared days and nights. They shared hopes and dreams. They shared the groans, the grind and the glory. Mostly, we imagine, they shared the ups and downs of being humans: some liked one another immensely while others struggled simply to tolerate one another. And as they shared with one another, they shored one another up.

"Christian brotherhood is not an ideal which we must realize; it is rather a reality created by God in Christ in which we may participate," Dietrich Bonhoeffer said in *Life Together: A Discussion of Christian Fellowship.*[1] What does your corporate body of Christ look like? How does it help you grow of body and heart? And how do you do the same for others? We can trace the genealogy of the physical family to its origin, right in the Garden of Eden. Likewise, we can trace the spiritual family of God back to its source: God. Christ incarnated himself so that we would catch a whiff of heaven, of a Spirit-dimensioned kingdom life. In turn, we—individual bodies within the body of Christ—become mirrors of grace and hope to a physical world of isolation and brokenness.

All of us have a family, though not all of us have a healthy one. But in the beginning, God envisioned both physical and spiritual families as safe havens for communion with God. It is with this in mind that we ask: what does the larger "body of Christ" look like, and how do I, as an individual body, fit within that larger body?

Within your body of Christ, as you do life together, how might you focus on health and wellness?

TOGETHER FOR THE GOOD OF ONE ANOTHER

The choices I make in daily life for my body and heart affect others in the body of Christ, the church, at two levels: physical and spiritual. If I do not care well for myself, I have no wiggle room to be able to care for you. Yet, as rugged Western individualistic Christ-followers, most of us would take offense if someone made a comment about our physical body as connected to our spiritual life, because we view that as a private matter, not a communal one. To confront or confirm one another about spiritual matters of heart and soul is risky; to confront or confirm one another about bodily matters is often considered downright inappropriate. Yet the care of our body impacts how we care for the body of Christ, as Bonhoeffer notes:

> Every act of self-discipline by a Christian is also a service to the community. On the other hand, there is no sin in thought, word, or deed, no matter how personal or secret, that does not inflict injury upon the whole fellowship.[2]

The body that we walk around in every day plays a vital part in our role of following Christ here on earth. After all, this same body will be redeemed, renewed and restored fully one day. Most of us steward things like our cars and our computers better than we steward our bodies.

What conversation does the church need to help its members have to bring light to places of fear and darkness? If I am not eating healthy, not exercising regularly, yet I spend hours in service or in prayer, I am usually considered holy and healthy as a Christ-follower. However, my eating and exercising habits, or lack thereof, shed light on my interior life. Comfort foods are often considered no big deal. In reality, excessive comfort foods point to the fact that I am letting something (food) comfort me, rather than allowing Christ to be my source of true comfort. If I am

What are some specific ways you might begin to talk honestly about physical appearance and lifestyle choices with those with whom you fellowship?

slovenly in my treatment of my body, am I displaying some lack of inner discipline, revealing a layer of sin, a layer of doing-it-my-way-ness, that I would prefer not to be noticed?

Revealing our interior struggles, which show up on our exterior bodies, will require risk. Allowing another Christ-follower to spur us on, encouraging us to steward well whatever physical body—

malady and ailment included—we have been given, also requires
risk and trust. Christ, unafraid to give up heaven for such as us,
invites us to steward our body as a living sacrifice for God's glory
and for the good of the whole body of Christ. This may require me
to give up something in order to gain the status of one fully integrated in heart, mind, soul, spirit and body.

THE ROLE OF THE BODY OF CHRIST ON EARTH

We seek to be fully integrated so that we can be Christ's presence
in the world. First Corinthians 12:27 says, "Now you [plural] are
the body of Christ and individually members of it." In 1 Corinthians 12:12-14, Paul also uses the parts of a human body to describe the body of Christ. Each person in the body of Christ, that
is, the church universal, is important, just as each separate body
part is critical to the overall health of the human body. Ephesians
4:12 and 5:23, along with Colossians 1:18, 24 and 2:19 also use
this analogy.

When Christ ascended into heaven, we as corporate faith communities and as individuals became his hands and feet here on
earth. If a child needs teaching, Christ does it through one of us. If
someone needs healing, Christ works through health-care professionals and prayer warriors. If someone is hungry or naked or in
prison (Matthew 25:31-46), we, the larger body, are to meet that
person's needs. If a member of the body hurts, we the body ache
with them. We are called to weep with those who weep and rejoice
with those who rejoice (Romans 12:15). As our whole physical
body is impacted by an illness or injury to one part, so too is the
body of Christ. The church is meant to function organically.

My (Valerie) daughter spent part of her senior year of high
school living in rural Alaska as part of an exchange program. She
was far from home not only in distance but also in culture as the
bush of Alaska has little in common with urban Colorado. The
only access to this bush village was by plane or boat when the river

wasn't frozen. A middle-of-the-night call during her time there woke my husband and me up. A medical emergency required our daughter to be evacuated by air ambulance into Anchorage, three hundred miles to the east. Being only seventeen, the small clinic in the bush needed parental permission and insurance information to initiate her evacuation.

As it turned out, the emergency was not life-threatening. Strangely though, she was released from the hospital with no money or identification, no return plane ticket, and no shoes. It was November, a time of deepening cold and dark in Alaska, and we knew no one in Anchorage who could help her.

From two thousand miles away, I pleaded by phone with the hospital social worker for help with some of my daughter's basic needs. She had missed the only flight back to the bush that day. The social worker provided housing for the night in a hospital-related residential facility. Yet she was of no help with my daughter's lack of shoes and other basic needs.

In desperation, I reached out to the body of Christ. I cold-called a large, downtown church in Anchorage, telling the secretary my plight. Since I also work in a downtown church that gets many requests for assistance, some legitimate, some not, I assured the woman on the other end of the phone that I was not just "working the system." I would gladly reimburse the church for their help. The conversation shifted from wariness to a real desire to help with no repayment expected. Not only did this woman bring my daughter inexpensive shoes, she brought a goody bag filled with snacks, a comb, a toothbrush and magazines to keep her entertained. My daughter was blessed as we reached out

Where might you need to call on the larger body of Christ as Valerie did? What ways might you be able to offer help to those in need within the body of Christ?

to the larger body of Christ for help and that body responded by extending hospitality to a stranger.

It is an odd blend, isn't it? We are to take care of our bodies so that we do not become a burden on the body, and yet we are to go to that body when we need help. We are not to feel ashamed if illness or injury occurs; yet we are also to do all we can to prevent those illnesses and injuries. When the body of Christ is called on to help someone in need, we are to do what we can. Christ said that something as small as a cup of cold water given in his name in a time of need is given, in some mysterious way, to him. A toothbrush, comb and shoes fit that category as well.

We, the individual members of the body of Christ, are to be good stewards of our health, thus not creating unnecessary hardships on that larger body. We cannot be the hands, feet and voice of God in our homes, neighborhoods, schools and workplaces if those hands, feet and voices are exhausted or out of commission due to misuse. Moment by moment, every day, we make conscious or unconscious decisions that lead us toward health or toward disease. Our responsibility as Christ-followers is to seek to make healthy, God-pleasing decisions. We can ask ourselves, *How are my physical choices affecting not only my own spiritual formation but the formation of the body of Christ as a whole?*

There is a difference between those who struggle with chronic conditions, especially if they developed despite good attention to one's health, and those who developed medical conditions due to an utter disregard for maintaining God-given health. We are focusing on the latter here: the ill health that results from unwise eating habits, lack of exercise and other lifestyle

What choices did you make today that affected your health for good? For ill? Will those choices affect your larger faith community?

choices such as smoking or overindulgence in alcohol. Illness and infirmity leading to death will come to all of us eventually, but we are not to hasten it along through irresponsibility with the body God has given us. We are to live in such a way that we are not a burden on others, as much as we can control that.

Paul suggests in 1 Thessalonians 4:4 that we are to live a life that pleases God. Part of the holiness and honor Paul is talking about relates to the physical care of our human bodies. Yet, when our bodies are in trouble, James 5:13-15 says we are to reach out to the body of Christ. We are not to become isolated and ill through the desire to live independently beyond what is reasonable or safe, a desire that puts an unnecessary burden on the larger body of Christ.

A BODILY WITNESS

The idea that we are accountable for the choices we make that impact our body as well as our soul can be hard to hear or talk about. Reactions such as "Are you saying God doesn't love me if I am unhealthy?" are not helpful. Why were we created? To be Christ's presence here on earth and to glorify God through our lives. That belief invites us to take care of ourselves. Oftentimes, we are tired, overweight or in pain because of self-indulgent choices that were easy to make at the time. Yet, those choices can lead to hard situations, which may then rule our lives. The results are not God's fault. The poor lifestyle choices we make regularly have an impact beyond our own bodies. They impact our very witness to the good news in Jesus Christ.

Many think that witnessing about our faith only involves talking to people. While our verbal testimony is an important part of our Christian witness, God also invites us to live in such a way that those watching us see a life of joy and vitality. When we live with the false belief that a healthy level of caring for ourselves is selfish or narcissistic, we risk not being able to be fully present to another. Our exhaustion due to lack of care for our body and soul is not a good witness to the abundant life in Christ. Therefore, learning to like vegetables or exercising regularly can be viewed not only as a spiritual formation exercise for ourselves but as an evangelism tool as well. Seeing our physical health as integral to our spiritual health will not only help us be the better for it, but those around us may be intrigued by our joy and energy. They might even want to hear more about why we go to church or have a relationship with God.

A PLAY ON WORDS

The New Testament also uses "the body of Christ" to mean the elements used in Holy Communion, which is also called the Lord's Supper or the Eucharist. This expression, the body of Christ, originated in Luke 22:19-20, where Jesus refers to the bread and the cup as his body and blood. As we partake of the body of Christ, the elements of the Lord's Supper, with other members of the body of Christ, the church, we are united with others and with Christ himself. It is a mystery to be sure: by taking Jesus into our physical bodies, we are empowered to translate those elements into being Christ's presence in the world. A unity is created that transcends time and culture.

Once, while traveling in Jerusalem, I (Valerie) stumbled into a traditional liturgical worship service. The historic form of the liturgy that has been in use in the church around the world for centuries was being sung. The language was not one I even recognized. Yet suddenly, I became aware of where they were in the service: the portion of the liturgy that begins Holy Communion. I joined in, speaking the liturgical responses in English, including praying the Lord's Prayer with them at the appropriate moment. I can't think of a time in my life when I felt so much a part of the body of Christ through partaking of the body of Christ.

The joyous mystery is that in the body of Christ, the church, here on earth, there are millions of individual members, all working in ways that Jesus in his singular earthly body never could. Through the body of Christ given to us in Holy Communion, we are strengthened as individuals and as members of that larger body. Let us commit to being as healthy as we can be so that Christ's body here on earth remains vital and a joyful witness to wholeness and the fullness of the good news of Jesus Christ.

CLOSING PRAYER

Holy Trinity, you are three-in-one. Yet you each have individual personalities and giftings within your union. Look at us, this glorious and messy body of Christ that you call your church. Sometimes we as individual bodies trip up others and ourselves, causing all sorts of havoc in the larger body. I can so easily find flaws in the way my neighbors treat their physical bodies and yet so easily ignore how I care for my own. But you had something grander in mind, I think.

Jesus, John 17 records your prayer that we would all be one as you holy three are one. What in the world does that mean when it comes to physical body life within the spiritual body life? What can I learn from how you three care for and love one another? What do I do with my friend or my acquaintance who is taking advantage of the larger body of Christ by ignoring his or her own health and wellness? How might I come alongside someone who is neglecting their own needs yet using some of the rest of us to be a caretaker when we aren't fully responsible for their actions?

How does the gift of Communion, where we partake of your body and blood, Jesus, lift us to a new perspective of what the body means, and what we mean to the body?

Some of these Christ-followers are not easy to be around, physically or spiritually. Yet I know I'm not always easy to be around either. I make excuses for the extra roll I eat, and the extra roll it brings around my midline. But I'm quickly judgmental of others who are sadly out of shape.

What shape do you desire to see in us as individuals and as a larger body, Father, Son and Holy Spirit? What does the healthy body of Christ look like? How can I do my part to create health and wellness? It's mighty easy to grab a highly processed snack, fast-food item or quick-to-make-but-unhealthy dish to bring to the fellowship gathering. What might happen if I approached preparing food for our gatherings with as much care as I put into my time in your Word, being in your presence and in prayer? Is there a way I can begin to model healthy habits to those who struggle even more than I do with their body's shape and health? Could I agree to meet a friend regularly to walk and talk rather than to sit and eat?

You talk about how you came to set the captives free. How can we as individuals help one another be free of the tyranny of poor eating habits and lack of exercise? You remind us that you notice when we feed the hungry and the thirsty among us. Who is hungry for real food and real drink that will satisfy the physical body in healthy ways?

Help me care for my own body, and the bodies of others in the body, so that I, like you three-in-one, might be part of something bigger than myself. Stewarding wisely my body and encouraging another to do likewise is important, I think. Show me how to meet my fellow sojourners at the intersection of health and wellness of body as well as heart. Amen.

REFLECTION EXERCISES

1. Standing in front of a mirror, take an honest assessment of your body. What does your care for your physical being say about what you believe about God and about your body within the body of Christ?

2. Watching someone ruin their health through poor lifestyle choices can be difficult. Talking to them about it can be even harder. What might be some ways to start the conversation of

physical health and its relationship to spiritual formation in
your faith community? For example, is there a parish nurse
who could start a weekly small group related to fitness and
nutrition? Could Lent be a time for your faith community
to focus on the body and its role in following Christ? Find
someone with whom you can begin a conversation about
this issue, praying for God to guide you in the best paths for
your community.

3. For the next week, track your body actions: what you consume,
   when you exercise, rest, play, laugh, create. Where might you
   engage differently with your body, and how might that impact
   your heart with Jesus?

3

Our Body in Worship

With our body as well as our soul we can choose to live each day in worship. All that we become offers back to God reverence and thanksgiving for the blessings he bestows on us. This is the worship that occurs in the quotidian places of life, the everyday, ordinary moments, when a sunrise brings tears of joy, when that robin hopping on the back deck reminds us that we are infinitely cared for, when the simple laughter of a friend warms our heart. At such moments, worship wells up richly. This echoes Psalm 148, where the psalmist calls us, along with all creation, to praise our great and glorious God. Our heart offers a simple thank-you: for the phone call received from a favorite relative or an old friend, for a smile of appreciation, for the chance to savor the wonder of the blueness of today's sky. All of life can become a place of worship if we but turn our heart to attentiveness, seeing how we are graced each day by the Lord's lavishing love.

LOVE'S LANGUAGE

Alongside these simply profound ascensions of praise in our heart, how can we use this everyday body to worship this everlasting Lover of our soul? How is our body an expression of devotion within our everyday private moments of worship or during the times of corporate worship with the family of God?

After a thirty-four-year absence, my (Lane) high-school sweetheart found me again. Can you imagine the many stories we told, catching up on life across that chasm of absence? We talked and talked and laughed and talked and cried and talked. We asked questions; we began to dream; we wondered and wandered through those lost years in story. But, trust me, we did not spend all our time in deep conversation, or even in light dialogue. We walked hand in hand. We hugged. We lingered over goodnight kisses as we parted to go home. As our love reignited, our expression of love moved from our heads to our hearts, from our hearts to our bodies, from words to actions, manifestations of those words. We brought one another little gifts, sent a gazillion email love notes, and celebrated our love more and more intensely and intimately as we married.

What might be a new way to express your love to God through your body?

The same thing can happen as we worship Jesus. Love experiments with expression. It looks for a way to offer gifts of love to the lover. It looks for ways to offer variety in the gifts given. As I have grown in intimacy with Jesus, I have begun to explore new ways of showing him love, of showing him worship.

WORSHIP'S LANGUAGE

Across the expanse of our (Valerie and Lane) lives, we have each moved a variety of times. With each move came the opportunity to discover a new church home. We each became acquainted with a variety of worship communities. Such explorations nudged each of us to consider why we worshiped God in a certain way. As we moved from place to place over the years, new ways of worship and new postures of worship were added to our love repertoire. Worship is the act of adoration of God. It is expressing back to God what we believe about him, what we feel about him and how we see ourselves in relation to him. When we truly see God, we are in total awe, starkly aware of his vast holiness and our vast unholiness. Worship belongs to God alone, and we are invited to worship him with all that we are. "Worship, in all its grades and kinds, is the response of the creature to the Eternal," Evelyn Underhill said.[1]

What might happen if you tried out new ways to worship, using the body to express love for the present yet invisible lover of your soul? For example, you could try praying at home with your palms up when asking God for something and your palms down when you are releasing a situation to God. Or you could kneel by the bed to offer thanks to God for the day before going to sleep.

As you begin to experiment with new ways to use your body in prayer and worship, consider how you already use your body to communicate. When a loved one dies, tears, laughter, hugs and gentle touch at the funeral all offer a sweet remembrance of the one who died and hope to those still putting one foot in front of the other. Think of that little two-year-old who catches your eye at a family gathering. When he does a little jig, don't you join in the dance? What happens when your best friend makes you laugh out loud? Do you slap your knees or give her a quick squeeze or pat on the back? A colleague at work gets a welcomed promotion; a handshake or high-five ensues. At the sports event last week, you clapped and cheered with arms raised. The symphony's beauty brought forth rousing applause and a standing ovation. All of these bodily actions are

What bodily expressions are evident in your body of worship?

ways of celebrating, ways of offering, ways of comforting, ways of grieving, ways of connecting.

Within worship, whether private or corporate, body postures also offer ways to express ourselves to the Holy Trinity. Bowing our heads at grace over a meal or during the call to worship in a church service are likely fairly familiar body movements used within worship. Kneeling and standing are probably also somewhat comfortable to many who love Jesus. However, there are other expressions of worship that cause some of us to squirm a bit even at the suggestion. But we cannot deny the fact that others throughout the Bible and throughout history have tried out a variety of postures in order to express a plethora of emotions as they wrestle with, wonder about and worship God.

ENTERING THE WORD

We only have to reach for the Bible to see a variety of worship postures in the lives of those who adore God. Bowing, clapping, dancing, kneeling, sitting, standing, lifting hands, falling down with prostrate bodies—someone in Scripture engages in each of these actions at some point.

With the whole of our body, with the whole of our heart, we bow down before the One whom we adore. Psalm 95:6 invites us to come and worship, to bow down before God. Bowing down is a humble stance as we are awed by the holiness, mercy and grace that God pours down on us. We see Moses bowing down to God in Exodus 34:8 and David doing likewise in Psalm 138:2. Adoration of the Holy One and humility in the heart of the worshiper come together in this posture of worship. When we bow, we are surrendering our entirety to the eternal one. "I AM the LORD your God . . . no other gods. . . . You shall not bow down to them or worship them" (Deuteronomy 5:6-9). There is but One we worship.

The full extension of our body as we lie prostrate lays us bare to the One who can ease our pain, hear our cry and forgive our sins.

Joshua, David, Aaron, Moses, Abraham and the disciples all fell facedown before God, sometimes in awe, sometimes in disbelief, sometimes in supplication, sometimes on behalf of others. Seeing God clearly, we then see ourselves clearly. God is holy. God is good. God is powerful. God is sovereign. We see how God's heart toward us is for good, for delight, for holiness; we are both humbled and made aware of our great need for deeper intimacy with the Holy One-in-Three. With our face to the ground and our bodies stretched out either in supplication or worship, we notice afresh the bigness of God compared to the stature of our own body.

There are times when the people of God weep, while at other times, when God turns our tears to joy, we dance (Psalm 30:11). There is this deep sense of joy in Psalm 126, one of the Songs of Ascent, that those who are set free praise God with laughter and joy that permeates all of their being. Dancing is often the frolicking accompaniment of joy in the Bible. We see the promise of merry-making, joy and dancing in Jeremiah 31. The people, both young and old, dance in response to the loving-kindness of the Lord. In Exodus 15, Psalm 149 and Psalm 150, tambourines join the dance music as part of the praise to God. Remember how the whole house of Israel and King David danced with all their might before the Lord in 2 Samuel 6? Their joy could not be contained as they brought the ark of God to Jerusalem.

We use our hands to reach up and cry for help, to tell of our soul's thirst, to bless the Lord and to praise his holy name. In Psalm 28:2, expressing a need for God's mercy, David lifts his hands. Parched, thirsting for more of God and asking for mercy, David spreads his hands out (Psalm 143:6). Likewise in Psalm 88:9, out-stretched hands beg for a need to be met. This nonverbal communication shows what is going on deep within the one worshiping God. There is a sense of surrender in this upward and outward cry of the hands, a desire to receive and be filled with what God offers in response.

The emotions of our heart toward God can be seen in the stance of our body before God. When Peter healed the lame man, the man jumped up and began walking and praising God. With the limbs that were healed, he offered worship to the One who healed him. When our hearts are attuned to God, the body responds to the emotions within. Peter, in Luke 5:8, falls on his knees, aware of his sinfulness. Often we do likewise, as kneeling is a stance used for confession as well as supplication.

With our hands uplifted, we worship and bless the name of God. Like David and the sojourners in the Song of Ascents did, we can lift our hands to praise God (Psalm 63:4; 134:2). Though at times we tend to associate this gesture with particular denominations, throughout Scripture the people of God use their hands to praise, bless, clap for and adore God.

We use all that we are to take in all that God is. This attentiveness of heart manifests itself in the use of our body. As we worship through our reading of the Bible, verses such as Psalm 27:4 guide us: "One thing I ask from the LORD, this only do I seek: that I may dwell in the house of the LORD all the days of my life, to gaze on the beauty of the LORD and to seek him in his temple" (NIV).

We use our eyes to physically gaze on the beauty of the Lord as we look at creation and at the way the Lord creates beauty in each of us. We also imaginatively gaze on the Lord as we enter the words of Scripture. We visualize the scene set before us in God's Word: the smell of the sea, the grit of the dry dustiness as the disciples walked with Jesus, the joyous sound of laughter around a smoky campfire at day's end after the feeding of the multitudes, the hearty bread and salty fish gathered in baskets woven of local materials, the rough hands of these fishermen-turned-followers of Christ.

We inhale calm as we bring ourselves before God, following the invitation of Psalm 46:10: "Be still and know that I am God." We use our minds to meditate on God, like Psalm 48:9 invites: "Within your temple, O God, we meditate on your unfailing love" (NIV 1984). We are quietly attentive to the voice of the Shepherd, for as his sheep we know his voice (John 10:27). Interior spaciousness brings us in touch with God's presence (Isaiah 40:11; 41:3). Like the lovers in Song of Solomon 1:3-4, we inhale the essence of God's being. Then we offer back praise in prayer, incense that rises to our Lord (Psalm 141:2). Whether in the tasting of the words we read in the Bible or in the tasting of the Word in Communion, we are fed food that nourishes our heart, which in turn nourishes our body (Psalms 34:8; 119:103). Anticipating a celebration, we look forward to the wedding feast of the Lamb (Revelation 19:9).

In *Wishful Thinking: A Seeker's ABC*, Frederick Buechner notes, "Phrases like Worship Service or Service of Worship are tautologies." A tautology is a way of saying something twice with differing words. The way our body expresses what our heart believes and feels toward God seems like such a tautology. We express bodily the love within us to the Lover we adore. Buechner goes on to say that there are two basic ways in

If God were only to watch your body language this last week, what might your body tell of how you feel toward God?

which we worship: one includes doing for God what God needs done, while the other includes doing what we need to do for our love of God. To quote Buechner on this latter point:

> The other way is to do things for him that you need to do—sing songs for him, create beautiful things for him, give things up for him, tell him what's on your mind and in your heart, in general rejoice in him and make a fool of yourself for him the way lovers have always made fools of themselves for the one they love.[2]

Like those who have gone before us as recorded in Scripture, our bodies offer a language of love to God. Whatever "dialect" you choose, God understands the language you speak with your body and your heart.

A VARIETY OF OFFERINGS

It is with our mouth, our lungs, our tongues, that we ask, rejoice, sing, shout our love and our questions to the Father, Son and Holy Spirit. In some churches, people make the sign of the cross at various times in the service. This acts as a visible reminder of the Father, Son and Holy Spirit and the gift of eternal life given to us long ago on a far-away cross.

Muscles are strengthened through a variety of physical exercises. Love is strengthened through a variety of expressions. How we offer our bodies in worship to God can stretch and strengthen our expressions of love to the One who loves us most.

Consider also worshiping and praising God through your senses: see, hear, taste, touch and smell along with movement and breathing. A candle or incense during the liturgy or private prayers awakens parts of our body as we worship. A walk in the woods while listening to the birds or a nearby brook engages the whole body. Savoring the bread and the wine in Communion draws us deeper into the life of Christ. Using our hands to journal, paint, do a bit of carpentry or mold clay engages all of our senses in expressing our delight in God. Hold a rock and reflect on how God is the Rock of Ages. Inhale and think of inhaling the breath of God that gives you life.

When I (Lane) taught ESOL (English to Speakers of Other Languages), my professor would say, "You can't reach all the children all the time with the same type of lesson. But in every lesson, if you add some variety, you can reach every child." We are like those children: not every bodily expression of worship is going to reach us to expand our way of worshiping God. However, by trying a variety of worship postures, we are bound to find a new twist to the deep love we have for God.

There are many different modes of worship and connection with God. Worship, where we express our love to God for God, is as diverse as each of us. Some of us are more able to hear God when we are in nature. Some of us are more able to engage with God through acts of service. Some of us are contemplative. Others of us like more formal rituals. Expressions of love will spring from deep within. Much like giving a gift to a friend, if you always give the same gift, the receiver might wonder if you are fully awake, fully alive, fully attentive, or just going through the motions. Have courage and offer your heart; step differently into worship by using the body you have to glorify the One who gave you that incredible body.

Psalm 139 says we are fearfully and wonderfully made. From head to toe, let us use this wonderful gift of life to pay attention to our body. Then, let us also use every part of this God-given body to turn back and worship Father, Son and Holy Spirit.

CLOSING PRAYER

As I enter this time of prayer, Holy Spirit, free me to experiment with using my body to worship you. Help me, God, echo how your people have adored you with not only their hearts and souls but also their bodies.

Lord, your holiness makes me want to remove my shoes. I am on holy ground with you. The joy of your amazing love sets my feet a dancin' while my voice rises in song to you. I am aware of my need for forgiveness, and I bow and kneel. Stretching out on the floor, all of me is exposed to all of you. Here confession reminds me again that I am but dust. Sitting at your feet, I look up and see the love in your eyes.

I rise up, arms raised, in praise of your splendor this day. With all that I am, may I ever worship you. Amen.

REFLECTION EXERCISES

1. What new ways might you engage with your body to express itself in corporate worship? How might you encourage your place of corporate worship to try new bodily forms of worship?

2. Experiment in the privacy of your own home with different postures for prayer. For example, try doing your daily prayer time face down on the floor or with your hands raised shoulder height, with your palms up, or kneeling. Does it enhance or hinder your prayer time?

3. Examine the way you engage your body during your daily Bible reading and prayer times. What might be a new way to involve your body and senses more? Singing? Lighting a candle? Standing or lying prostrate to pray?

4

Toward a Balanced Lifestyle

Here we get to the heart of the matter; it is where much of the tension lies as we look at the question "Is the physical body and its health relevant to spiritual formation?" Let these words wash over you for a minute: Dr. Stephen R. Covey, borrowing an idea from the twentieth-century Methodist missionary E. Stanley Jones, has written, "While we are free to choose our actions, we are not free to choose the consequences of our choices."[1] We can choose what to eat and how to use our body, but we will not be free of the consequences of those activities. We can smoke, drink alcohol excessively, use illegal drugs, or misuse prescription and over-the-counter medications, but at some point, the consequences to our body will not be under our control anymore. Mouthful by mouthful, minute by minute, day after day we are moving toward greater health or disease.

For years, I (Valerie) resisted fully practicing what I knew about eating well, such as eating little to no refined sugar and no artificial ingredients, and exercising, for example taking a brisk thirty-minute walk four times a week. I knew all about the warnings of what happens when one is fairly casual about good nutrition and intentional movement, but since I was healthy, at a good weight, I didn't worry about long-term consequences too much. Then I hit my mid-forties. Suddenly, in the throes of perimenopause, my body no longer responded the way it used to. I was often tired and began to gain weight more quickly than the one or two pounds a year I had been gaining. My hormones were like a roller coaster. My previous mouthful-by-mouthful choices and lack of regular physical activity had come back to haunt me. Slowly, often with gritted teeth, I began to heed the gentle nudgings of the Holy Spirit to change my eating habits and to exercise. Suddenly the need for more vegetables and more intentional movement each day became very real.

I discovered, as many others have, that it is much harder for most of us to lose weight than to gain weight. It is more difficult to move muscles that haven't been pushed for years than it is to keep youthful muscles toned into middle and old age. I resisted simple things like brisk walking or light weightlifting exercises because it was easier to come up with a reason not to do those things. The irony is that when I was feeling tired, a brisk walk, a Pilates class or a bike ride would have energized me far more than the caffeinated soda or candy bar I grabbed out of convenience.

But do not be discouraged! I also discovered that transitioning slowly to wise eating choices and beginning an exercise program can make a difference no matter how old you are or what state your physical health is currently in. I began to eat something green at each meal. I learned to exercise regularly, in my case daily walking with Nordic poles that function as light weights, through an American Heart Association program that rewarded my little "hash marks" for each day's movement level with a T-shirt at the end. (A bit of incentive or a competition of some kind can be a great motivator!) I substituted whole grain flour for white flour in everything I could, and I began to drink more water. As the saying goes, I did what I could and not what I couldn't, discovering as each month passed there was more in the "could" category than the "couldn't."

Our bodies are remarkable at healing themselves if we will but give them good food, regular exercise and enough sleep. Adults need between seven and eight hours of sleep a night. Brisk walking for thirty minutes three or four times a week as well as eating the recommended five servings of vegetables and fruits with lean protein (half your weight in grams each day) are goals many of us can achieve in a few weeks. I am pleased to report that after several years of intentionality, my body is responding positively. I have more energy and feel good. I am at a better weight and have mitigated some medical problems that had begun to arise.

At the cellular level, God has designed our bodies to seek health. Think of the last cut or bruise you had. A healthy body gets to work right away healing that injury while we go about our day. Isn't it miraculous how a small injury like that disappears in a few days? Even bigger health problems can also be lessened or even turned around. For example, many books and websites show conclusive evidence that diabetes cannot be cured but can be reversed.[2] Heart disease, joint pain, lung damage from smoking—a discussion with your health care provider will give you tools to "turn back the clock" in some areas. Noticeable improvement in health can happen within a few weeks of making changes toward a diet that consists of foods found mostly at the perimeter of the grocery store as well as walking at every opportunity during the day along with other lifestyle changes, like smoking cessation programs.

IF WE KNOW THESE THINGS, WHY DO WE DO THEM?

We have all kinds of rationalizations for what are ultimately unwise choices: "Calories don't count on vacation," or "My dad smoked for years and never got lung cancer." These rationalizations show the level of denial we are capable of. First Corinthians 6:19-20 asks us: "Or do you not know that your body is a temple of the Holy Spirit within you, which you have from God, and that you are not your own? For you were bought with a price; therefore glorify God in your body." Glorifying God in our body means, among other things, keeping it as healthy as possible.

Think about your last meal. What would Jesus say about it? Was it healthy, natural food that honored the Holy Spirit in you, or was it highly processed, that is, altered significantly from its natural state or even created in a laboratory?[3] Did you even eat, or were you so busy that you grabbed a soda or another cup of coffee? Mealtimes, complete with time to chew, reflection on your day so far, and time reorienting yourself to God through a short prayer, feed our souls as well as our bodies. Those times are gifts from God to us and we are invited to treat them as such.

If you are not sure what a "real meal" includes, the Choose My Plate website (www.choosemyplate.gov) illustrates what a healthy dinner plate looks like. For example, a plate for a "real meal" would be half fruits and vegetables. Half of all the grains on it would be whole grains, such as a whole-wheat dinner roll or brown rice. The protein would be lean, like a grilled chicken breast.

Shopping for healthy food comes before making healthy meals. A site that can help you make good choices at the grocery store is: http://summertomato.com/how-to-find-real-food-at-the-supermarket-flowchart/. The site provides a fun chart you can download and take to the store. The humorous questions and diagram can guide you through the store with its myriad of choices.

How did your last meal fare against the guidelines suggested above? What is one change you might make in your next meal?

Reflection exercise 1 at the end of this chapter has tips in helping you transition to a more wholesome diet.

Moving our body on a regular basis is also a critical piece of a balanced lifestyle. For example, many of us find it easy to drive everywhere, but the price we pay for that convenience may lead to the loss of joint mobility, core strength, balance and muscle flexibility. The cliché "Use it or lose it" applies not only to brain function but also to body mobility. Exercise programs such as swimming, aerobics or Pilates classes offered at the YMCA or health clubs are excellent options. Yet daily movement can also be as simple as taking the stairs rather than the elevator, walking instead of driving a short distance, or parking as far from the door as possible. One health program advocates walking 10,000 steps a day. Those 10,000 steps do not have to be taken all at once. By walking down the hall to speak to a work colleague instead of sending them an email, you can accumulate a lot of movement in a day quite easily. Try using the restroom that is furthest from your office. That will get you extra steps, movement that adds up to more energy and a better weight. An inexpensive pedometer can help you track how many steps you take each day, showing you what your activity level is now and giving you a healthy goal to work toward.

The Global Corporate Challenge (GCC) partnered with Lancaster University in England to "study the impact that increasing daily physical activity has on the physical and mental health and wellbeing of employees across the world."[4] Their results validate that healthy choices lead to happier, more productive lives:

> The extensive study found that the British Gas employees who participated in the GCC reported significant increases in their concentration levels at work, enhanced enjoyment of day to day activities, an increase in overall confidence, a higher level of general happiness/wellbeing and a greater sense of self-esteem.
>
> While these findings are remarkable for both the wide ranging positive effects and the specific level of increased wellbeing, the most impressive result of this increased wellbeing was a significant increase in their productivity at work, their engagement levels at work and their job satisfaction levels.
>
> The study also looked at an employee's sources of stress at

work and it was found that through their participation in the GCC employees reported a decrease in stress levels. This included both the stress relating to overall wellbeing and stress from their lives outside of work (i.e. family life).

The conclusion was that GCC participants were happier, healthier, more productive and dramatically more engaged with their work and employer as a consequence of their participation in the GCC.[5]

Every human resource department manager or head of a household may want to find ways to help the people in their care live a more balanced lifestyle based on these findings.

SELF-CARE IS A GODLY ACTIVITY

Why do we let ourselves get to a point of ruined health when all along we could be making better choices? There are many reasons. Often they fall under the category of "lack of self-love." Some Christ-followers have been raised to think that caring for themselves is bad or selfish; everyone else's needs always take precedence over their own. They skip meals or grab fast food on the run, stay up late night after night just to "get it all done," and are then surprised to find themselves in the back of an ambulance having a stroke or heart attack.

On a scale of one to ten, with ten being the best, how would you rate your overall self-care?

Self-love is not the same as self-indulgence. We are the temple of the Holy Spirit, not only collectively as Christ-followers but also as individuals. It pleases God when we take care of his temple. Self-love comes from wanting to care for the body that God has given you. This is not sinful but rather a sign of wise stewardship. If this is a difficult issue for you, find a spiritual director or another trusted friend who can help you see where the line between self-care and self-indulgence may be for you. It will not look the same for everyone.

Many years ago, I (Valerie) knew of a pastor's wife, probably only in her fifties, who "ran herself into the ground." She was the one who always said yes, always volunteered to help or bring a casserole and never put her needs ahead of anyone else. She developed a chronic condition, which required her to rest, which she chose not to do. Twice, she nearly died. Finally, her health ruined, she was forced to take disability. Often, we are guilty of subtly encouraging our pastors, youth workers and other church leaders toward workaholic lifestyles. Is there a clergy person or other staff member at your church who needs to be encouraged to take their day off or to take their full vacation? Church workers are often the worst at modeling good self-care. We can help them understand that they will serve God and the people under their care better if they are rested and taking care of their health.

Do you recognize yourself in the story above? All of us struggle with "old tapes" that play messages of putting others first or "work for the night is coming," as the old hymn says. Somehow, the idea of simply "being" with God, enjoying his presence, doing nothing but sitting with him while watching a sunset, seems "sinful" or wasteful. Yet God is the consummate lover of our souls and longs for a relationship with each of us in the same way lovers here on earth long to simply be together.

The irony is, the more frantic our lives are, even in the service of God, the less useful we are in the kingdom of God. There may be times to "run a horse into the ground" if you are being pursued by an enemy, but it is not the normal way to enjoy horseback riding. So it is with our bodies, the home and transportation for our souls during our time on earth. With the power that we receive from leaning into God's power, we can accomplish what God put us on earth to do and still care for ourselves physically, spiritually, emotionally and mentally.

We cannot be the hands and feet and heart of Christ if those body parts are suffering from neglect or even abuse through overuse. We are God's beloveds, and our bodies will be redeemed in the resurrection along with our souls. It behooves us to take care of both. A healthy body will help the soul be healthy and strong; a healthy soul will help the body be strong and healthy, a circle that reinforces each part.

If your body were the only thing you could use to communicate God's goodness, what would it say right now about your life?

In Romans 12:1, Paul appeals to us, "by the mercies of God, to present your bodies as a living sacrifice, holy and acceptable to God, which is your spiritual worship." In some mysterious way, our bodies themselves are a form of worship to God. We are his creation, which has been proclaimed as good even though fallen. As such, we are called to use our bodies to worship God, as we noted in chapter three. Part of our Christian witness as God's creation is to be healthy, strong and living well in the body that God has given us.

BALANCING ALL THE FACTORS

One of the consequences of the Fall as seen in Genesis 3 was a loss of balance. When people were no longer allowed to live in the Garden of Eden, an environment perfectly suited to their needs with face-to-face communication with their Creator, they lost the ability to always make the right choice. With sin in the world, humanity naturally fell into bad habits based on ease and convenience. Anyone who has raised children knows that instilling a disciplined lifestyle, which promotes good health and life-skill habits, is often an uphill battle.

Additionally, there is the issue of genetics, conditions that we are predisposed to due to heredity. Too often these become scapegoats, places of blame for why we are overweight or why we cannot walk around the block anymore. While genetics do play an important role in our health, especially as we age, pick up any magazine these days and discover that genetics do not have to have the final word in many cases. Research shows that we can eat our way into diabetes and heart disease. An inactive lifestyle may end with a stroke. Even some of the chronic conditions like multiple sclerosis, Parkinson's disease, and Alzheimer's now show signs of responding to a natural foods diet (lean protein, lots of fresh fruits and vegetables) and regular exercise, such as swimming or brisk walking four times a week. Many times, making these kinds of changes has been shown to lessen the severity of the symptoms of the disease. Sometimes a predisposition to one of these conditions can be delayed through diet and exercise. For example, Christian K. Roberts and R. James Barnard, from the Department of Physiological Science, at University of California, Los Angeles, California, state:

> Currently, modern chronic diseases, including cardiovascular diseases, Type 2 diabetes, metabolic syndrome, and cancer, are the leading killers in Westernized society and are increasing rampantly in developing nations. In fact, obesity, diabetes, and hypertension are now even commonplace in children. Clearly, however, there is a solution to this epidemic of metabolic disease that is inundating today's societies worldwide: exercise and diet. Overwhelming evidence from a variety of sources, including epidemiological, prospective cohort, and intervention studies, links most chronic diseases seen in the world today to physical inactivity and inappropriate diet consumption.[6]

All of this may seem like another burden in an already overstressed life, but adding guilt is not our goal. Rather, we want to be an encouragement to you in living a long and healthy life. Just as a longtime heavy smoker should not be surprised when diagnosed with lung cancer or emphysema, neither should we who have not really taken care of our bodies be surprised at diminishing health as we age. As tempting as it may be to assign blame to God, most of us recognize that these diagnoses are not God's fault. God loves us and longs for us to live full, healthy lives. Even when we struggle with a congenital or chronic condition, God longs for us to make the best choices with food and movement we can each day. He is gracious and loving and will never abandon us, even if we make choices that lead us to illness, injury or an early death. God will be sad, but his love for us will never change.

The good news is that we can take responsibility for our physical health choices day by day, sometimes even minute by minute. We have the power right now to stop some diseases and illnesses before they become chronic conditions. Through prayer and with the help of our doctor and spiritual director, we can change the old messages we have been living with into words of wisdom and health. Think about your current food and lifestyle choices. Will they lead you into a joyful, healthy old age, or will they contribute to increasing aches and pains as each year goes by? With the free will God has graciously given to all of us, we can make changes starting today that will lead to joy and health in the years to come.

A place to begin might be to approach each meal as a "Eucharist" (another name for Holy Communion that means "thanksgiving" in Greek). Doing that may help us not "eat ourselves sick," a very telling expression. Instead of dieting or swinging wildly between overeating and starving ourselves, we can aim for a balanced approach to food. For example, we can enjoy the piece of cake at the birthday party but then the next day forgo sugar and other empty calories to balance out the cake. We can stock our refrigerators with precut carrot and celery sticks, making it easy to grab a healthy snack. We can walk more, appreciating not only God's creation but also the miracle of our bodies with their myriad muscles, joints, tendons and ligaments all working in harmony without conscious effort. Choosing an apple over a candy bar could become a small way of saying to God, "I want to take good care of the temple of the Holy Spirit you have given me."

We did not become unhealthy overnight, and we will not undo a lifetime of bad choices quickly. However, mouthful by mouthful and step by step, we can begin to give glory to God with each meal and every movement. We can use our physical choices as much as our spiritual choices for the glory of God.

CLOSING PRAYER

Lord, I enjoy food. The sweet tart redness of a raspberry wakes my mouth up. The crunch of a carrot feels good in my mouth. Thank you for the smell of cinnamon, the color of peaches, the taste of beets roasted in my oven. Thank you for Genesis 1. You created so many wonders and declared them good. I love that you made food. I agree it should be declared good. What joy it is to savor a good meal with old and new friends. I'm mighty glad you made water, too. It quenches my thirst on a hot summer's afternoon.

But, God, sometimes I'm on the go—a day full of meetings and errands. Quite frankly, on those days I'm lucky if I remember to eat. Sometimes, when I haven't gotten to the store, nothing looks appealing except the junk food that is left from that gathering I recently attended. If we are on the road, headed out to explore or visit, it's not all that easy to eat healthy or exercise on the go.

I wonder how I can reboot my balance meter on days like that. How could I, listening to your voice of encouragement, be more intentional about planning toward health and wellness?

Sometimes exercise can seem like a chore. When I was a child, being active was not considered "exercise"; it was just playing, just being a kid. We would roam the woods, kick a ball around, jump rope, climb a tree and shoot some hoops—whatever was fun to do outside. There were many summer evenings when my parents had to call me several times before I would hop off my bicycle and come in for the night. Is there a way to recapture some of that playfulness through exercise today? What would a playful, healthy engagement with exercise be like?

You tell me to become like a child. I wonder, do you also mean to be more active, like when I was young? I imagine you and Mary and Joseph were often out walking together. Did you run races with other children who lived near you?

Lord, help me recapture a childlike wonder toward food and exercise. Let me savor that which nourishes my body, that I might offer life to the fullest to others as well.

Amen.

REFLECTION EXERCISES

1. "Edible" and "food"[7] are not necessarily the same thing anymore, due to the use of chemicals in many agricultural practices as well as the processing many ingredients go through before they make up the final product. (The website http://darinsnaturals .com/food-and-nutrition/ might be helpful to look at if this is a new concept to you.) Take one meal and analyze it. Separate out, as much as you can, how much of it is "food," that is, things found in nature (grown in the ground or on trees, or an animal protein source that has not been altered significantly), and how much of it is "edible," that is, ingredients created in a lab. You may need a dictionary to look up some of the words in the list of ingredients. Including all seasonings, condiments and beverages, what percentage of your meal was "food" and what was "edible"?

2. Do you know what your Body Mass Index (BMI) is? This is a tool that can be used to determine if you are in a healthy weight range or are overweight or even obese. You can quickly calculate your range at www.nhlbisupport.com/bmi/. While this is just a tool, albeit a useful one, it is not the only measure of health. For example, you may fall into a normal weight range

but not be healthy overall for other reasons. People who are thin may be that way because of not eating regularly or because of thyroid issues. See your health care provider and discuss your BMI number. Ask them for suggestions on how you can improve your health through exercise and proper food choices.

3. Warning: This website may scare you into good health! See www.dailymail.co.uk/femail/article-2051161/What-TWO-glasses-wine-day-face-years.html. The site offers computer-enhanced pictures of a woman's face ten years from now if she keeps smoking, drinking or eating excessive sugar. If these are habits you struggle with, use this website to encourage you to overcome them. If you are a man, you can still get a good idea of what happens to the body when not well cared for from this site.

5

A Theology of Food

We believe that Christ-followers can be continual witnesses to the goodness of God through the way we approach food. What might this involve? We can begin by spending our food dollars to support sustainable farming practices,[1] local, organic growers, and meat and dairy producers as much as possible. We prepare that food in ways that keep the nutritional values high, such as not overcooking vegetables or adding a lot of sugar to naturally sweet fruits. We encourage mealtimes that, after a prayer of heartfelt thanks for God's provision, are slow-paced enough to enjoy the food and conversation. We advocate "food" and not "edible."[2]

We can branch out by supporting fair trade options, in which fair prices are paid to producers in developing countries for the items we cannot get locally, such as coffee, olive oil or chocolate. If we feel called to do so, we can write to our legislators locally and in Washington, D.C., lobbying for laws that will support the earth, farmers or issues related to healthy school lunches for all. We could, if we felt called, tackle the issue of "grocery store deserts," those areas of the country where the only place to buy food is a convenience store. We can pray about starting a local food and produce cooperative in one of those areas. We could discuss the idea of using some of the church's property for a community vegetable garden as a way to help needy neighbors.[3]

The issues of agribusiness, hunger, slow food, and organic and local movements are complex and multifaceted. It is impossible to do them justice in a short chapter. There are widely varying opinions surrounding these issues, and not all terms are clearly definable. For example, *hunger* in a discussion like this can also include the politics of food distribution. While some may hear overtones of Paul's statement "those unwilling to work will not get to eat" (2 Thessalonians 3:10 NLT), it is important to not take it out of its original context. What seems like a straightforward, biblical solution quickly dissolves under the realities of getting food to hungry people, often in hostile environments. Many times, a mere scratch under the surface of an issue opens up a multilayered cavern of far-ranging problems with no easy solutions.

Briefly defining a few terms will be helpful. *Hunger* refers to food insecurity of any kind, including a lack of water resulting in famine. *Agribusiness*, or corporate farming, has become derogatory shorthand for ways of growing and processing food that involve the extensive use of chemicals. It often implies a misuse of the land as well. The Slow Food movement (www.slowfood.com) is the antithesis of agribusiness, focusing on ways that honor food from creation to consumption. "Organic," a relatively new phrase, advocates the support of farmers who do not use pesticides or genetically modified seeds. "Local" means the food source is within a one-hundred-mile radius of where the consumer buys it.

Appendix C resources at the end of the book barely scratch the surface of all that has been written on these topics. We encourage you to look at what is listed there and read further. Not all suggestions are written by Christians, and some may be controversial, but all have something to say about the issues in this chapter.

So why do we even attempt to tackle this? Because in reality, food is not neutral. Not only does food affect the health and wellbeing of those who consume it; it also affects the health and well-being of those producing it. The politics of food distribution are complex, even insidious at times. The farmers who grow our food struggle to make ends meet. Migrant farm workers are often exposed to high levels of toxic chemicals from the fertilizers used on the fields. Multinational companies send their processed food all over the world, sometimes to the detriment of indigenous populations. One example is baby formula disrupting the breast-feeding cycle in Third World countries, especially in areas without access to clean water in which to mix the formula. All of these examples are part of a network that affects every person on the planet. What we put in our mouths is ultimately a statement of what we believe about God, ourselves and our neighbor, making food a theological issue.

We can extend our awareness to the earth's water sources as well. Pastor Ben Stewart writes:

> Our bodies are wondrously a living part of the earth. This connection sometimes turns ominous: springs, aquifers, and drinking water all over the world now flow with detectable levels of pharmaceuticals. What we thought we were putting into our own veins now flows through the veins of the earth. . . . What we have put on the earth now flows through our bodies, even to our breastfed infants. When human bodies come to worship, the earth comes with us, in our veins, in our bones.[4]

The build-up of chemicals on the land from use of heavy fertilizers, which then runs into our rivers, streams and oceans, is showing up in our tuna fish sandwiches. Other fish sources are being depleted or decimated by careless commercial fishing practices. Whole species are endangered from mismanagement. Is this what God intended when he gave stewardship of the earth to Adam and Eve and their descendants?

Another area of discussion has opened around genetically modified organisms (GMOs), which are relatively new on the agricultural scene. They are viewed as either saviors or villains and are quite controversial. The long-term effects from these types of modern industrialized farming practices are not yet fully understood, but the initial research is not favorable.[5] Where will we as Christ-followers take our stand on these issues?

FOOD AS A THEOLOGICAL STATEMENT

We do not intend for this to be a guilt trip in any way, especially if this is new information to you. These concepts are simply statements of another level of the physical world intersecting with our spiritual formation. In this intersection between the body and the soul, we seek to serve our neighbors at home and abroad, as much as possible, by supporting healthy and sustainable agricultural and animal husbandry practices. It can be as simple as buying food from a local farm stand or farmers' market. This can be a way to live in remembrance of the poor either as an individual or through your faith community if it commits to addressing some aspects of these issues. It is a matter of social justice. It is a way we say yes to the food God created for humanity to eat in the Garden of Eden.

Honoring God with our food choices does not mean eliminating all canned goods and prepackaged foods, as some may fear. It does not mean we all have to grow

Take one food item and trace it from your table to its source. What did you learn?

and preserve our own food. It does mean being intentional with our food dollars. Generally, when shopping for premade foods, the fewer the ingredients, the healthier the product is. If you cannot pronounce or understand what some of the ingredients are, the item is suspect, regardless of any health claims on the package. It means seeking out animal products that have been humanely raised. Creation is for our use, not our exploitation.

With every bite we put in our mouth, we are making a political and theological statement. With our approach to food and eating, we proclaim what we believe: about God, our bodies, the care of the earth and those who harvest food from it, and the poor. This is not to say there is one right answer regarding how we eat or acquire our food. Some will answer the call to be vegan; others will be responsible hunters. This is part of what spiritual formation is about: putting ourselves in a place where God can form us to live as we were created to live.

All of us can ask the butcher or store employees if the food in our grocery cart has been treated humanely since birth or grown with sustainable practices. Does the fish and seafood we are buying meet the Monterey Bay Aquarium Seafood Watch criteria?[6] How might we develop a relationship with a local grower or producer?

Do you agree with the statement "every bite we put in our mouth is a political and theological statement"? Why or why not?

There are things we can do to make a difference. Often, it starts with a simple question about a food item's source.

While we may not be able to completely avoid consuming food that impoverishes someone else in some way, we can seek to minimize doing that. Businesses are sensitive to how people "vote with their dollars." If people do not support certain agricultural practices and quit buying the products produced by those practices, companies will change their ways. For instance, if every family quit buying soda pop[7] and sugared breakfast cereals, which negatively affect our health, or decided to buy only food that had been ethically produced, corporations would take immediate notice and seek to make changes. Never doubt the power of your grocery dollars and what you can do with them for good.

It is important for our faith communities, and not just us as individuals, to reflect an awareness of God's creation and our food supply. Leslie Leyland Fields shares that church potlucks are often the worst places for finding food that reflects the goodness of God's creation:

> It's potluck Sunday. . . . I have some idea of what the offerings will be: hot dogs wrapped in white buns . . . buckets of drive-through fried chicken anchoring the table. Neon-orange cheese doodles will inevitably show up, somewhere near the salads. The greenest item will be several bowls of lime Jell-O with fruit suspended in it, which, I've decided, is to signal its inobvious function as food. We pray our thanks over this smorgasbord of chemical wizardry and marketing genius, ask that it would strengthen our bodies (something I believe will take divine intervention), and invite Jesus to be among us as we eat.[8]

Does this describe the food at your church? How do we go about gently making changes as a community without offending someone who has brought an offering of food?

When I (Valerie) was much younger, but old enough to know better, I foolishly blurted out a negative comment about the canned bean sprouts used on a dish at a potluck. While my desire for fresh may have been a valid concern, I offended the woman bringing it in irreparable ways. As we learn to approach food in ways that reflect God's goodness more deeply, we must always seek ways to approach the issue with sensitivity to those around us.

Making changes as a group takes careful planning. Does your church have a parish nurse or a fellowship committee? Perhaps a conversation with them about ways to educate your congregation about some of these issues is the place to begin. Start small. If your congregation serves doughnuts with the Sunday morning coffee, add fruits and vegetables to the fare. Gradually reduce the doughnuts, substituting whole-grain baked goods. Encourage people, without

making them feel guilty, to bring healthy offerings to church potlucks. For example, could they bring a grilled chicken dish rather
than a fried one? Could they bring a vegetable platter instead of
potato chips? Do this in a
spirit of love, not judgment.

Some congregations are
developing relationships
with wheat farmers and
vineyards for making
bread and wine/grape
juice for celebrating the
Eucharist.[9] *How might*
your faith community do
something like that?

Promote it as an attempt at
group awareness to the fact
that eating and food have
wider implications than may
seem obvious at first. Lent is
often a good time to explore
new ways of fellowshiping together as many are aware of
giving things up for forty days
in preparation for Easter.

DO NOT BE DISCOURAGED

It is so easy to spiral into guilt or hopeless despair because of these
complex and seemingly insurmountable issues, leading us to
denial or purposeful avoidance of the whole issue. In reality, it is
easier in the short run to simply buy what we want in the grocery
store without examining every ingredient or tracking down every
source. Yet, in the long run we can make a powerful statement by
what we have in our grocery carts. Also, we can pray regularly for
those who grow and harvest our food, often under difficult conditions. Where possible we can prayerfully seek ways to bless the
soil, to build up fish populations and to be good stewards of the
earth God gave us. It may seem like such a small thing to buy a
free-range chicken instead of a factory farm raised one. Yet even
small things can have big consequences in the kingdom of God.
For example, Jesus changed the world with only a dozen close disciples. Our small steps in seeking to honor God through our food
choices can add up to big changes over time.

Another place to begin developing a greater awareness of the theology of food can be during our own mealtimes. How often do we multitask while eating: grabbing lunch at our desk at work[10] or while running back and forth between the kitchen and the laundry room? How many times do we mindlessly ingest food, only to wonder why we are still hungry an hour later or are gaining so much weight? In our rush to "be productive," we too often forget how to simply *be*. We view our food with the same detachment we have toward putting gas in the car. Food is for pleasure as well as sustenance. It is not a necessary evil to be ingested quickly with the least amount of preparation as possible. Food is a gift from God to strengthen our bodies and spirits, to be shared in community. When we neglect to eat with thanksgiving and intentionality, in the company of family and friends when possible, we may feel deeply unsatisfied in body and soul.

Which area do you need to address first: the purchasing of food or the eating of it?

Percy Dearmer wrote a poem, often sung as a hymn, called "Draw Us in the Spirit's Tether." His third stanza is a prayer for us to learn to make our life and our meals into sacraments to God. Serving others is one way he suggests we can live sacramentally.[11] If we can find ways to make our meals "sacraments" that feed our bodies in the same way the Eucharist feeds our souls, we will have another way to witness continually to God's grace through creation.

How each of us will respond to the political and theological implications of buying, preparing and eating food depends on many factors and much prayer. There is no one-size-fits-all answer, though there may be some overarching principles. However you choose to respond to the concerns in this chapter, do so out of love for God, love for your own body and love for your neighbor. That will make a difference no matter what side of the issue you land on.

CLOSING PRAYER

I walk through the grocery store and am overwhelmed with all the choices. Even as I think that, I realize that there are places in my own town, state and country, as well as overseas, where people have no choices at all. While I am overwhelmed with a plethora of options of what to eat and what not to eat, there are others who go hungry this day.

I also know I live in a country where free enterprise and business opportunities have created the conglomerates of corporate farming. I like oranges even when they are out of season, so I too contribute to the transportation of produce from thousands of miles away. And often the things on sale are not fair trade options or local or organic. The chemicals and antibiotics impact not just my body but also this earth. But foods without them are mighty pricey.

Sometimes, it would just be easier not to be a thinking, caring Christian. Yet, Lord, you gave me a mind to think and a heart to wonder and be concerned for others. So I wonder, Lord, what does stewardship of my eating look like, in light of so many complex factors?

Sometimes it feels weird increasing the amount I spend on groceries for me, when others have no resources at all. Other times, I think that if I don't take care of my own health, I won't be much good for anything, like caring for and serving others.

Jesus, how do you want me to lean into responsible eating? I've never really thought of myself as being politically astute, but maybe all this information about food has to do with something even bigger than me. You, Jesus, continually went up against the establishment when the things they did diminished the goodness of God.

This is all befuddling to me, Lord. Would you help me sort this all out? I want not only the words of my mouth but the food that I put in it to be something that brings glory to you and also allows me to be mindful of caring for my brother and sister in other circumstances across the globe. Amen.

REFLECTION EXERCISES

1. Is there a CSA (Community Supported Agriculture) option near you? This is a program that many smaller farmers have where you "buy" a share of their farm and in exchange receive regular boxes of produce from them. If that is not an option, search out farm stands or farmers' markets you could support. Alternatively, find a local farmer and purchase some of their produce, eggs, meat and/or milk.

2. Do research to discover what fruits and vegetables are in season in your area. For example, what is considered in season in June in Florida is going to be different from what is in season in Montana then. For a week, try to eat only fruits and vegetables that are currently in season in your locale. Besides being fresher, they will probably come from a source that is closer to where you live rather than from hundreds, even thousands, of miles away. Those long-distance transportation charges all add up to the final cost of the product and its environmental impact.

3. Go to a convenience store. Walk the aisles and plan a week's menu from the food options in that store. How healthy would you be if that store were your only source for food? There are children and teenagers in America who have never had a fresh vegetable or piece of fruit as there is no grocery store for miles around. The only place their families can get food is at an over-priced convenience store. Do you feel called to be an advocate for such a situation? The website http://freshmoves.org/about talks about someone trying to solve the problem of a grocery store desert in Chicago.

6

Questioning Cultural Messages

*A*rt, *literature, music and the media have* influenced and reflected our perspective of the body over the centuries. Think about the changes since your parents' time, let alone your grandparents' generation. If we look even further back, we see more changes. Just as there are trends and fashions in clothes, home furnishings, cars, even kitchen appliance colors, so we find periods of art, music, dance and theater that are so distinctive they can be categorized by name. For example, the art of the Baroque period (1600–1750) is very different from the art of today. Gregorian chant is different from the music played by "praise bands" in many churches. Some have argued that the medium is really the message, that music, for example, is a Trojan horse for the message of the lyrics. Whatever the medium, the truth is that what we are surrounded with each day, what we watch and read and focus on, forms us, for good or for ill.

Consider the contrast between the portrayal of women as seen in the paintings by Rafael, the Italian painter (1483–1520), and the mid-1960s British model Twiggy. An Internet search will lead you to photographs of both. In Rafael's paintings, women were full-bodied, even voluptuous. Twiggy, on the other hand, promoted a very thin, almost genderless-looking body as the ideal. Compare Michelangelo's 1504 sculpture of David, a paean to the ideal man, larger than life and perfect in body form, to Alberto Giacometti's 1949 *Three Men Walking*, figures of average height, featureless and emaciated-looking. In their day and age, each portrayal reflected attitudes toward the body.

Old television shows and movies reflect a shift in the portrayal of women in the 1960s and 1970s. Prior to those decades, glamorous movie stars tended to be full-figured. During this shift, women became significantly thinner, with a "boy's" body, clothed in pants, suit jackets and the traditional men's neckties. It was as if women did not even want to look like women anymore, out of fear or disgust at being viewed as a sex object instead of being seen as a beautiful, intelligent person of significant worth.

Recall Jackie Gleason's 1960s television show. A portly Jackie would sit on stage in his smoking jacket with a cocktail in one hand and a cigarette in the other, the model of a male who had "made it." Ben Cartwright, the father on the TV series *Bonanza*, though a robust outdoorsman, still had a bit of stomach hanging over his belt. In complete contrast to these earlier barrel-chested men, today's male media celebrities are muscled and lean.

Today's runway models and Hollywood celebrities, both men and women, achieve impossible looks through extreme fasting and plastic surgery, displaying body shapes that are unhealthy and unachievable for most people. Pre-adolescent and adolescent girls are left with an impossible task if they aim to look like the model on the cover of a magazine. Many die, figuratively if not literally, trying to achieve this unrealistic and unhealthy look. Ironically, according to U.S. Surgeon General Dr. Regina Benjamin, the average American woman is actually gaining weight, coming closer to the ideal of the time when Raphael and Michelangelo lived.

It is as though women know deep down that what is being shown in the media is unattainable and even wrong for anyone trying to live a healthy lifestyle in the body shape and size they were given. I (Valerie) remember a time with two friends. We were the same height and wore nearly the same size in clothing but weighed very different amounts. One of us was big-boned, which made her much heavier on the scale than the much smaller-boned one of us. If we all had tried to weigh the same because of an artificial standard set by some modeling agency, two of us would have been very un-healthy. We often fail to remember that someone who is very thin may have gotten there by starving himself or herself or through an eating dis-order. Eating well, at the appropriate number of calories recommended for your gender and age, will lead to a healthy weight and glow.[1]

How comfortable are you with your body as it is right now?

ALL MEDIUMS CARRY A MESSAGE

We are bombarded everywhere with the "ideal" man or woman. They are of impossible slenderness with surgically altered or oth-erwise unhealthy physiques and airbrushed appearances. Mixed messages abound. Men are told to be "Ralph Lauren tough" while getting in touch with their "softer side." Despite years of feminist ideals, most women's magazines still focus on weight loss and diets that include all the chocolate cake you can eat. Men's magazines use sex appeal to sell everything from cars to suitcases. No wonder so many feel so confused and disconnected from their own bodies! Who and what are we to believe?

Never doubt that the role models we are exposed to day after day through popular culture mediums influence the way we view others and ourselves physically and, by extension, emotionally. During the formative middle and high school years, teenagers can be scarred for life physically, emotionally and spiritually from negative feedback. Such messages received, directly or indirectly, from peers, teachers and even parents linger long past the teen years. Boys, who often finish their growth spurts well after high school, feel tremendous pressure to compete with the looks and abilities of other males who have matured earlier. Girls often aim for a certain look, rather than for a healthy body appropriate to their build.

Music, art, literature, drama and dance surround people of all ages with mirrors: an image of the artist's view of God, or no God, as well as humanity's perspective at that moment. Bombarded constantly with visual images, song lyrics and advertisements, these messages subtly impress on us what we are or are not to be and how we should look. With wisdom and discretion, we need to discover for ourselves, as well as teach children, what those influences are carving into our heart, body, mind and soul. We must translate or transform cultural messages into truth about how we are to care for our body and for each other.

For instance, do the lyrics and video images teach men to respect women? Do the cultural messages teach women to respect themselves? Do we know that there is an unconditional Lover who created the universe, one who knows us so well that even the hairs of our head are numbered? Luke 12:7 and other such verses can change our perspective of ourselves from what the culture tells us to what God intended for us.

Additionally art, music, dance and theater offered within our faith communities ideally become a manner of learning and leaning into biblical truths, rather than taking on the culture's subtle messages, which work against such truths. We are to be thinking Christians, taking every thought captive to Christ, then living that out in our daily lives and these everyday bodies.

However, even the church isn't free from current cultural influences. Sacrificing theological integrity for the lyric's rhyme scheme or to fit the melody often puts incorrect images of God and people

deep into our hearts and minds. Likewise, our worship spaces say
to the world what we believe about God and ourselves. Art, drama,
dance—all of it can be used to praise God and lift our hearts in
worship, but we must be careful, especially when children are
present, that the art form is reflecting accurately the truth of who
God is and who we are within creation. We cannot allow lies to
penetrate into the deep recesses of our spirits no matter how catchy
or "relevant" the tune, words or images may be.

Notice that genres or styles have not been mentioned. That is
because they are simply vehicles to carry truth or untruth. There
are "traditional" hymns that are not theologically accurate and
there are "contemporary" musical pieces of all types that pro-
foundly speak God's truth. It is the same with all art forms, from
fiction to dance and music to drama or any of the visual arts.

CULTURE IS NOT NEUTRAL

So what are we to do with all of these cultural messages with which
we are constantly bombarded? As with all of life, we are invited to
test the spirits behind things (see 1 John 4:1). We can recognize the
power art forms have to convey a message, true or false, deeply into
our soul. For example, how many times has a story that you read or
watched stuck with you for months, even years? Maybe there is a
song that has a special meaning to you that you have known since
childhood. Art forms add "sticking power" to messages. That is
why they are used in worship services, propaganda campaigns and
to teach children the alphabet on *Sesame Street*.

The film *Paradise Road* is based on a true story of women interred
in a Japanese prison camp during World War II. Two of the women,
one a trained musician and the other a Presbyterian missionary,
taught the others to sing the instrumental parts to several classical
pieces, which they sang on Christmas Day 1943. Betty Jeffrey, who
survived the internment, said of the experience: "When I sang that
vocal orchestra music, I forgot I was in the camp. I felt free."[2]

I (Valerie) remember a dark, gloomy day when my mood matched the weather. Suddenly I heard the most amazing music on the radio. My spirits were instantly lifted, and I was able to do the dreary task in front of me with a lighter heart. Art is transformative, for good or for ill. It can bring healing to the creator as well as to the observer. It can also reinforce ugliness, heresy and hatred.

By surrounding ourselves and the children in our care with influences to counterbalance those that popular culture presents to them, we ensure that culture's images do not subtly hijack the gospel message. This usurping can even happen in worship services under the guise of "being relevant" or "reaching the unchurched." That does not mean we have to sing German chorales every Sunday, but it does mean that everything we do, say, watch or sing in worship must be carefully scrutinized. We cannot assume that just because a Christian wrote it, it carries gospel values. With people's tendency to be constantly "plugged in" to electronic devices, always listening to something, we need to be aware of whether that "something" is making us a better disciple of Jesus Christ or undermining that effort. The discipline of celebration acts as a counterweight to subversive messages (see appendix A). Philippians 4:4-8, on which this discipline is based, charges us to think about these things, which include truth, honor and excellence.

As children watch television, advertisements and movies, or play electronic games, how can we teach them to discern that these are fictionalized situations, meant to entice or induce us toward an unseen goal? We can enjoy popular culture yet aim to infuse our body, heart and mind with God's realities and truths. Telling bedtime stories, reading from a favorite book, and Scripture-based prayer can be especially important here. Our minds process words and images through the night, even if we are not aware of it. Ending the day with truth and blessing is also calming.[3] We can take in theater and art shows, concerts and dance presentations, then mindfully discuss what was portrayed. Did it sync with God's Word or did it present an alternative message?

Wisdom is always vital, as not everything billed as "Christian" is safe or helpful. Many people who claim to follow Christ may have, usually unintentionally, false views of God and the workings of God's kingdom or humanity. Discernment in listening to and observing artistic works that are labeled "Christian" is critical. Skewed views of creation and the Creator by Christians are possibly even more damaging than those that make no claim to following Christ. People often let their guard down during things that are billed as "Christian" and fail to see subtle heresies being portrayed. Though constructed by well-meaning artists and musicians who are honestly seeking to follow Jesus, the art or music itself may not be solid ground on which to build an accurate theology.

What form of art speaks most to you in worship? What is the most distracting?

Yet, art, music, drama and dance can all be used to form us into the ways of Christ, even if they aren't overtly Christian. For example, the movies *Chocolat* and *Babette's Feast* as well as Mark Schweizer's novelette *The Christmas Cantata* all portray artists of various kinds bringing healing to people and places. These stories of redemption show broken people using their gifts and talents in ways that, in the end, help others to see God in new ways and bring healing to the artists themselves.

Story is a powerful medium; Jesus used it to show truths of the kingdom in his parables. Music brings words deeper into our soul than the spoken word is usually able to do. A picture, sculpture or film really is worth a thousand words. Movement teaches our muscles subconsciously. There is even a field of psychology that deals with "muscle memory" as a form of healing.[4]

Navigating all the cultural messages we take in daily is a matter of paying attention, of not going through life unaware and uninformed. As God tells us through 1 Peter 5:8, "Be sober, be vigilant; because your adversary the devil walks about like a roaring lion, seeking whom he may devour" (NKJV). Satan, the prince of this world (John 12:31) has his hands on many forms of art, music, theater, literature and dance, those labeled Christian as well as those that are not. We need to stay grounded in our faith communities and use prayer and Scripture to be able to detect those fingerprints. Art, literature, music and dance are gifts from our creative, artistic God. They are an integral part of our spiritual formation. May God help us to create works that lift people into the kingdom of heaven with truth, integrity and a creativity that mimics our Creator God.

CLOSING PRAYER

Your creativity is everywhere in your world, Lord. There's never a moment when we aren't surrounded by it. Our senses delight in smelling, touching, tasting, hearing and seeing all that you have created. You delight us with artistry that springs up from within people. We marvel at art, music, theater, literature and media that offer beauty of sight, sound and touch.

Sometimes though, Lord, the artists forget that they themselves are your workmanship, your *poiema,* from which we get the word "poem." A poem is a little bit of mystery that causes us to pause and ponder. As your *poiema,* God, we are created in Christ Jesus to do good works, which God prepared in advance for us to do, as Ephesians 2:10 reminds us.

As we explore the ways creativity is displayed in the world, make us wise to discern what is good and godly that will lead us toward holiness, and what will trip us up. Our bodies are good and holy vehicles for our souls. May we find ways to enjoy creativity that display bodily goodness, while knowing that you are the artist from on high. May all that we inhale by our senses draw us deeper in love with you. Amen.

REFLECTION EXERCISES

1. Take an inventory of your house. What kind of art do you have hanging on the walls? What music plays frequently? What kind of books and magazines do you read regularly? What kinds of movies or TV programs do you watch the most? Ask yourself: do these things give me a better picture of who I am and who God is, or do they work against the Holy Spirit in my life and the lives of those who live with me?

2. Think back to your last corporate worship experience. List all of the music, art, dance and/or drama used in the service, if any. What were the messages, explicitly and implicitly? What did they tell you about God, about humanity, about creation, about the kingdom of God?

3. Dorothy Sayers was a Christian who wrote murder mysteries. J. R. R. Tolkien, also a Christian, wrote the *Lord of the Rings* trilogy. Read one of their books. If you did not know they were Christian, would there be hints in the story that might cause you to suspect they were?

7

Extremes Examined

Consumerism fuels our economy. Affluence is often touted as the goal. Even in the midst of an economic downturn and flat economy, we continue to shop.

Often the values of the culture subtly become our underlying values. As a matter of fact, we not only pay attention to the culture's notions of what matters, we run after these notions as if they were the ultimate prize. Even as Christ's followers, we gulp down the messages the culture serves up, especially when it comes to how we view and treat our body. The culture espouses extremes, and we don't even blink. We take the culture at its word, aiming to echo rather than question the ideal body.

Our culture encourages attainment of a certain bodily form when it comes to looks: lean and muscular for men, willowy and winsome for women, the six-pack abs for men, the concave belly for women. In reality, we do not just desire a certain look or fashion; we worship it. We worship the body in ways bold and subtle. Plastic surgery may be one form of body worship. Extreme exercising and dieting are also evidences of ways we bow down to the body. Fashions are meant to accentuate what is beneath the clothing. However, often models mold our thinking about how our bodies should look more than the types of clothes we should wear. We live looking at the outside first and desiring a particular shape and size more often than we care to admit.

Even as Christ-followers we are easily swayed to consider the body first and foremost when meeting a new person, or even when looking in the mirror. There is a tension that exists. How might the shallowness of looking only at the exterior reflect the shallowness of our own interior? At the same time, there is value in considering how our appearance might hinder the words we say or the life we live for Jesus if we are in some manner offensive in how we dress or look. It is wise to ponder these issues from varying angles. In the end, we arrive at a place of decision. We walk a tightrope between wisely stewarding our body, being wholesome and appealing to others, yet not wanting to worship the body we inhabit.

In an age of global media access, the weight, height and breadth of a person's body is displayed across the world in a matter of moments from an iPhone, iPad, television screen or movie set. The old adage "One can never be too rich or too thin" is taken as gospel truth, and values once held firmly are set upside down. In past eras when lack of food resulted in early death or easy contraction of disease, a portly body was viewed as a sign of success and wealth. Today, increasingly muscular men and increasingly thin women are often viewed as those with the most desirable bodies or are deemed to be successful and rich.

BODILY EXTREMES REFLECT A STRUGGLING SOUL

However, we need to honestly admit that something has gone askew when a person's weight is an extreme of either kind: too thin or too heavy. It can be an indicator of the struggles going on within the heart. For example, a person with no self-discipline may indulge to the point of obesity. We used to call this addiction gluttony, one of the seven deadly sins. On the other extreme, there are those who allow their body to be eaten away by the illnesses of anorexia and bulimia. Understanding the multilayered reasons and emotions beneath these actions is vital for gaining freedom from such bondage of body and heart. Exercising to the extreme displays yet another form of unhealthy body and heart integration. Peter Kreeft reminds us, "Gluttony is self-indulgence, the demand to have the world's real food for the stomach and the world's false food for the soul."[1] These disorders are not ultimately about food but rather about trying to distract oneself from difficulties of one sort or another. Often they arise in situations in which people feel they are not in control. Creating a particular pattern of eating or exercise as an attempt to regain some order gives a sense of control. Dr. Wendy Dickenson, a licensed psychologist, notes, "Excessive exercise becomes the norm, and restrictive or binge eating becomes a daily practice. It is typical for these behaviors to become more extreme over time." What lies at the core of these behavior extremes differs for each person. Dr. Dickenson explains,

> While emotions, the context, or relationships can feel unpredictable, rituals around eating and exercise bring a sense of control. When one senses that they have little or no power in their life, a sense of mastery over their behavior decreases feelings of powerlessness. Feelings of danger or vulnerability can be combatted by a perception of being invisible (extreme under-eating) or unwanted (extreme over-eating).[2]

One young woman who has journeyed through an eating disorder shared that the road from onset to recovery can take years. For her, it took both outpatient and inpatient care to combat the cyclical addictive behavior and to grasp the underlying beliefs that held her body and heart captive. Though she knew she was "killing herself" with such choices, she "bowed and submitted to the god of the toilet," even naming her illness "the adultery in which I engaged." She knew she was in desperate need of help yet was inconsistent in her commitment to get it. The gods of false beauty and false identity engulfed her. One day, though, God called forth her true beauty and deep substance, and she received healing and freedom. Such wooing by this true Lover of her heart kept those false lovers at bay.[3]

Recovery from a body extreme is as multifaceted as the reasons and expressions behind the disorder. As Dr. Dickinson explains,

These interventions need to address behavior patterns on a physical, emotional, cognitive, and usually spiritual level. Physical goals may include identifying new coping strategies, breaking behavioral patterns and reflexes, and learning healthy eating/exercise habits. . . . It is critical to one's recovery to develop a new or stronger sense of self, which can be argued is at its core spiritual in nature. Finding a sense of meaning, purpose, and strength for life is vital as one moves away from distractive patterns towards a healthy, integrated life.[4]

A good self-discovery starting point is asking God to help you see any unhealthy ways you may be trying to distract yourself from deeper issues. If you find that any body extreme is becoming an issue for you, bring this struggle to God and seek professional help from a counselor, physician or nutritionist, while also involving friends, family and even a spiritual director. If you are not sure of the difference between healthy weight control and an eating disorder, go to www.helpguide.org/mental/anorexia_signs_symptoms_causes_treatment.htm.

Extremes seem to many of us quite severe. Often we can't really identify with such behavior. Yet I (Lane) would be the first to admit that at times in my life, I have caught glimpses of those out-of-control habits. I imagine you have as well, if you'll stop and think about it. Who hasn't sat down with a bowl of popcorn or a bag of chips or cookies and, while watching an old movie or catching up with an old friend, suddenly experienced chagrin upon realizing your swift consumption of more than you had intended to eat?

After Thanksgiving feasts or other festive occasions, how many of us have groaned in bloated agony due to overindulgence and under-vigilance? Restaurants today serve portions that would easily be appropriate for two or three meals, yet we mindlessly eat as we chatter with friends. Moments of stress, deadlines at work, sudden crises that arise or even caring for those that are ill offer us opportunities to delve into unhealthy eating and exercising patterns. Running late for work or staying late at work or at the hospital when someone's sick, we stock up on a steady supply of caffeine and sugar, hoping to keep the energy aloft long enough to push through the tasks at hand. The same circumstances can lead us the other way; forgetful of food, we linger too long at the computer or in a meeting, then eat nothing at all to sustain us. In the end, extremes can nip at our heels, even if only for a few short hours.

Hypervigilance around food and exercise—or anything, for that matter—regardless of whether the extremes are on the healthy or the unhealthy side, is evidence of deeper interior struggles. In striving for some level of "perfection" or control in a particular area of life, our perspective becomes skewed. The focus on perfection leads us to be judgmental. We judge others or ourselves too harshly, forgetting the simple joys of food and exercise. Gratitude gets lost in greediness to be exactly correct. Rather than experiencing wholesome pleasure, we are controlled by pickiness. Celebration of the ordinary wonders of food and body vanish.

Orthorexia is yet another type of extreme. People struggling with it avoid foods they perceive to be unhealthy to the extent that they can become malnourished.[5] This is an attempt to eat well gone completely wrong. A health coach described a client with orthorexia this way:

> She had read pretty much every nutrition book out there and absolutely prided herself in the fact that she ate no contaminated foods. She had lost friends because of her beliefs around

food. She told me once that a friend went out of her way to make this woman "healthy" chocolate chip cookies. This friend made sure every ingredient was organic, even the butter! To which this woman replied, "Yes, but did you microwave the butter to soften it?" The answer was yes. So this woman refused to eat the cookies, saying that her friend learned a good lesson and wouldn't do it again next time. I'm sure there was no next time.[6]

People with orthorexia may extend their obsession to how the food is prepared, as evidenced by the story above. Each person needs to decide where the line is when it comes to eating nutritionally. Though both of us aim toward nutritionally dense and healthy food when cooking at home or eating at a restaurant, this aim is easily set aside in a variety of situations. Giving and receiving hospitality is a priority when food and friends are involved.

CHANGING OLD TAPES

It is true that many of our beliefs, false though they may be, originate in our family of origin as well as from the culture and era in which we were born. We both grew up in a time when cleaning one's plate was the ticket to being excused from the nightly family dinner table. "There are children starving in China" was the cajoling cry when one lingered too long with undesired food still remaining on the plate. "Your mother's slaved away making your dinner, so don't waste it" was another saying bantered about. Surely you can think of other mottos that you readily accepted as a child, which still, to this day, may be influential sources in your response to food.

Because we heard certain philosophies espoused by the adults around us during childhood, we assumed the words were true. As adults, we are wise to critically examine those childhood values. For instance, some of what we learned may result from what those of a previous generation learned. Those of the Depression-era generation often grew up during a time when a piece of fruit once or twice a year was considered a luxury. So when they reached an age of maturity in a land of affluence, overeating was not considered bad. Instead it was considered a sign of arrival. Rather than accepting the assumptions from the past, an attentive life ponders messages surrounding the body, which may lead to a realignment of our health beliefs and habits.

Perhaps one key is to understand the idols that sway us. Sin is anything that masters us. We are tasked to ask the questions: What is mastering me? What is eating at me that is driving me to eat

What assumptions and messages do you cling to that are related to your body? Do they align with what God says about your body?

or not eat to such radical extremes? To understand the desire beneath the desire, the message that drives us to false places, often undergirded by false mottos we have believed, enables us to see what is affecting our interior heart and soul, all the while being displayed in our quite visible body. This is a very clear intersection of our physical body with our spiritual formation. These strongholds may hold us apart from holiness and godliness. For example, only eating local and organic is a worthy goal unless it keeps you from fellowshiping with others who do not eat that way. Even something as healthy as exercise can be taken to an extreme. These lines are often hard to delineate or discern. But freedom comes not from eating what we want at any given moment, nor from starving ourselves into illness in order to look better. Rather, it comes from viewing food as one part of a wholesome and holy life.

CULTURAL MESSAGES ABOUT THE BODY

Additionally, world history and the history of the church have further influenced our view of the body. In the fifth century, Christianity became the official religion of the Roman empire. While this ended the persecutions, it also made the church more susceptible to the blending in of non-Christian cultural influences to its proclamation of the gospel. From the fifth through the fifteenth centuries A.D., people's view of the human body and the material world slowly shifted from a Hebrew understanding of creation's inherent goodness as made by God to that of an evil to be denied and risen above. This included a gradual succumbing to the Platonian division between body and soul, with the body being seen as base and expendable, while the soul was seen as the only entity worthy of one's time and interest.[7] This gradual shift led to all kinds of abuses of the body.

For example, St. Francis of Assisi (c. 1181–1226) called his body "Brother Ass," believing that it was to be subdued and beaten into submission to the "higher" realities of the spirit and soul. While there is some truth to St. Francis's view of the body as an unruly animal (rampant self-indulgence is not healthy for the body or the soul), this view was taken to such extremes that many, especially in the monastic communities of the Middle Ages, shortened their lifespans significantly through extreme fasts, self-flagellations and other forms of overly vigorous mortifications. If you read the religion section of your newspaper or are familiar with Dan Brown's *The DaVinci Code*, you are aware of Opus Dei, a modern group with elements of that extreme view of mortification.[8]

In the fourth century, St. Anthony fled to the desert of Egypt to escape the corruption he saw happening in the church, due to the legalization of Christianity under the emperor Constantine. Following Anthony's model, asceticism developed, characterized by abstinence from various sorts of worldly pleasures with the aim of drawing closer to God. The original root of the word *ascetic* comes from an ancient Greek term that simply means practice, training or exercise. In the Bible, we see examples in Jesus' life of both strict asceticism, such as his forty-day fast in the wilderness, and a wholehearted enjoyment of life, as when he made forty gallons of wine for the wedding in Cana. John the Baptist was called to an ascetic lifestyle before his birth. The angel told Zechariah that his son, who was to be named John, was never to drink wine or strong drink (Luke 1:15). As an adult, John lived in the desert, dressed in camel skins, eating locusts and wild honey (Mark 1:6; Luke 1:80).

In the early days of this monasticism begun by St. Anthony, the desert fathers and mothers, as this fourth-century group came to be called, often lived austere lifestyles, refraining from sensual pleasures and the accumulation of material wealth. Some would fast for forty hours before the Easter vigil service, the original Easter service that begins in the middle of the night. Later, that was stretched to fasting most of Holy Week. Some ate only on Saturdays and Sundays or every fifth day during Lent.[9]

Gradually in the West, the asceticism understood by St. Anthony and his followers changed from meaning a disciplined practice to something even more severe and rigid. Practices such as fasting and chastity, meant to help one love Christ above all else, came to be viewed as practices necessary to earn one's salvation. The Protestant Reformation rightly spoke against this heresy of works-righteousness but then swung over to the opposite extreme. Many Western Christians came to believe that one is saved by faith alone, as promised in Romans 3:28, which Martin Luther and others used to confront heretical practices in the Western church. However, this precious promise of being saved "by faith alone" came, over time, to be functionally translated as "I can live however I want to, because Jesus loves me and covers me with his grace." It is unfortunate that from the good of the Protestant Reformation, the pendulum swung to the other extreme. Both inside and outside of the church, being "good and moral" is, even today, equated with being Christian in some circles. The truth of how we are called to live is somewhere in the middle.

The call to be in the world but not of it is still valid. John 17:14-16, Romans 12:2 and 1 John 2:15 all speak to this idea. A Christ-centered life includes caring for our body as well as our heart, knowing that they will both be redeemed, made fully whole and fully holy in the life to come. We press into resolve, allowing the Holy Spirit to move us toward a well-balanced life, with rhythms of rest and work, creativity and stillness, quiet and fellowship, that we might find more freedom. We take Jesus' yoke as described in Matthew 11:29 because as humans we will always be following a master of some kind. Jesus has promised us rest when we are yoked to him.

We seek to separate out the goodness of the desert life shown to us by the desert fathers and mothers and translate it into our time and place. We say no to the excesses of our culture as the desert fathers and mothers tried to say no to the excesses of their culture. We do this not so that we can save ourselves from eternal separation from God but so that we can be good and faithful servants here and now (Matthew 25:23).

As we begin to examine the origin and reality of unhealthy body habits, we then, through guidance and healing from the Holy Spirit, start the process of becoming whole, while undoing our unwise ways. As we see what is eating at us, what is causing us to eat or not eat, exercise or not exercise, we press into holy dialogue with God, taking every thought captive to Jesus. We turn our thoughts into actions, setting our lives in holy and wholesome rhythms that move us toward health and wellness of body and heart. We are not to be always feasting, nor always fasting, but to find a healthy balance that integrates our exterior life and our interior life in such a way that sin is not our master. By so doing, the only extreme we will then have is the extreme passion of loving Christ above all else.

CLOSING PRAYER

"It is for freedom that Christ has set us free. Stand firm, then, and do not let yourselves be burdened again by a yoke of slavery" (Galatians 5:1 NIV).

"The thief comes only to steal and kill and destroy; I have come that they may have life, and have it to the full" (John 10:10 NIV).

"He has sent me . . . to proclaim freedom for the captives and release from darkness for the prisoners" (Isaiah 61:1 NIV).

Lord, I read your Word, and I read your life. Over and over again you offer freedom of one sort or another. But Lord, I wonder. Were there people who couldn't see that they needed freedom? And because they couldn't see their prison, they never asked for freedom? What are the prisons that keep my body stuck? What does it take to see and hear where there are barricades that prevent me from being fully integrated of body and soul?

I tend to think that things happen because I muddle things up or don't make enough of an effort for change to occur, or because I wrongly believe that some things can never change, so I give up before I ever start. What I forget is that I have an enemy, and he is determined to curtail your glory at every point. Your Word says that my body can reveal your glory. I don't tend to think of my body as a battlefield, but perhaps it is, Lord. Would you reveal my blind spots? Would you give me courage to raise my ostrich-like head out of the sand of avoidance? Would you give me strength to battle my enemy?

How might the armor described in Ephesians 6:10-18 help me in the battle for a healthy body? You exhort me, in Hebrews 10:23-25, to "hold unswervingly to the hope we profess" (NIV), while reminding me that in order to receive the encouragement and spurring on of others, I need to be in fellowship with people. Lord, too often I forget I have an enemy. Yet also I have fellowship. I have you. Lord, let me see the bars that hold me back from being fully whole and holy of body. Then come, as only you can do, Lord Jesus. Set me free. Amen.

REFLECTION EXERCISES

1. Self-flagellation is the act of a person whipping his or her own body with a switch or rod. We think of it happening in the

Middle Ages in strict monastic orders, but it can be found in some places today. Negative mind "tapes" are a form of self-flagellation. Reflect on your eating and exercise habits. Spend some time journaling about the negative thoughts that go through your head each day about yourself. Ask God to show you where those come from and to heal them by replacing them with God's view of you.

2. Reflect on this quote:

> If you don't have some touchstone to find your name in God, to find your identity in God, to find your food in God—that there's One who feeds you—then you are going to end up living in a revolving hall of mirrors. And everybody else's opinion of you, moment by moment, is going to be your only food. . . . If you can stand before the mirror of Jesus . . . and be reflected rightly by the mirror of God, that frees you from the revolving hall of mirrors, then you are letting the Bread of Life really feed you your life.[10]

Stand in front of the mirror, preferably nude. Ask God to show you what he thinks of your body. Ask him to help you let him be the touchstone for your identity and not what others reflect back to you.

3. What magazines do you read regularly? What are the messages in them about the body, especially in the advertisements? Consider taking an ad and "talking back" to it, out loud. Identify its message, and if it is not a godly one, speak back to it, naming truth. When we say things aloud, we are often better at hearing the truth or falsehood being portrayed. For example, a notion in our mind that seems right may sound false, and even ridiculous, when spoken out loud.

8

The Body Gone Awry

Our elementary school faculty meetings usually took place in a large cavernous room, as the one-hundred-plus elementary teachers and staff needed room to sprawl out. We formed a large circle in order to see and hear one another. One cloudy winter afternoon, most of the agenda centered on a few presenters seated near my (Lane) end of the room. As faculty meetings go, this one was rather interesting, so I was fully engaged with the topics at hand, not daydreaming or making mental lists as we all do from time to time in meetings. Then the focus shifted away from my end of the circle. A few minutes later, I noticed that all of those one-hundred-plus pairs of eyes were staring at me. My colleague nudged me. I looked at her quizzically. She nudged me again then quietly said, "Lane, the principal asked you some questions and we are all waiting for your response." I thought she was joking and said so. With that, the person on my left confirmed my neighbor's remark. "What do you think about the principal's questions?"

Stunned, I asked my neighbor to repeat the questions, which I then proceeded to answer. Apparently our principal responded, and though I could tell her mouth was moving, I could not hear any of the words she was saying. My neighbors helped me muddle through. The faculty meeting drew to a close. Afterward, the principal called me to her office. If you have ever been asked to report to the principal as a child, let me assure you, it does not feel all that different when you are a teacher and the same thing occurs. However, with kindness and concern, she requested that I set up an appointment with an audiologist immediately. I was glad to do so, thinking I would prove her wrong—there was nothing wrong with my hearing. I was sitting near the heater that cold winter afternoon. As far as I was concerned, that was the only culprit.

I could not have been more wrong. Tests confirmed it. I did indeed have a hearing loss. A bevy of tests plus a physical history of my body and life ensued in an attempt to chase down any possible cause for loss of hearing in a fortysomething-year-old. Cause: not known. No tumor. No accident. No loud rock music or accidental explosion going off near my ears. No industrial noise at work, unless you count the chattery cacophony of elementary-school students! A significant hearing loss was the reality. I did nothing to cause it. There was nothing I could have done to prevent it. But regardless of cause or, in my case, non-cause, my world shifted when a basic body function ceased to function appropriately.

My immediate plea to God was, "God, seriously? Seriously, God? A hearing loss? Now? Now in the midst of reeling through the most stress ever? Now during this unwanted divorce and its proceedings, endless attorney fees, raising three teenagers on my own, on a teacher's salary? Now, Jesus, really, now, here in the midst of college tuition and tight finances as an again-single woman, I'm dealing with a hearing loss? Lord, really, this is a bit much." The fear of the unknown seized me, threatening to capsize me. Fear of complete hearing loss, anger at one more thing to deal with, questions about hearing aids and concerns that they might still stymie my interactions with others flooded in. Health problems hamper hopes. They test beliefs previously untested. The jumble of my emotions poured out to God, echoing many feelings in the

Psalms. I wrestled with how to trust when doubt was an easy chair to sink into for a while. I cried. I pondered. I hoped I would wake up and this would all be a bad dream. Eventually, comfort and gumption came forth as I leaned deeply into the Holy Spirit's hovering among the chaos.

My daughter's tender response was, "Mom, I'll learn sign language if you completely lose your hearing. You know, this also explains that skewed response you had not so long ago." My tears from her heartfelt first words gave way to laughter from both of us, mutually recalling my interpretation of something she'd recently said. Walking through the den one evening, I'd heard her talking to a friend. With a quizzical look on my face, I'd chimed in, "Who are y'all talking about when you say, 'You're pretty but you're bald?'" Gales of laughter engulfed the two teenagers. When they finally recovered enough from their tears-in-your-eyes, doubled-over-in-laughter session, my daughter giggled and said, "Mom, my words were 'You're unbelievable.'"

My sons recalled that they'd noticed that the volume of anything electronic had increased—stereo music, car radio and television—while I barely noticed softer sounds. Together, we realized that communication had been increasingly frustrating. I would often mishear a word or would repeat a rhyme to their original word as my hearing loss was in the high frequency range. Perhaps the loss had been going on for a while, but it had taken the faculty meeting to bring it to the forefront of my attention.

Regardless of how large or small the event or the source, a body that goes awry creates havoc, doesn't it? It impacts not only the person whose body goes awry but also people in relationship with that person: family, friends, work colleagues and possibly even strangers. Adjusting to hearing aids was like learning a new language. The devices are marvelous in many ways, but the reality is that nothing can replace the way God created the healthy ear's capacity to hear. It took practice to learn a new way of communicating: listening more intentionally, placing myself in more conducive environments for hearing others and educating both myself and others about this new way of living each day. As these things go, it has been an interesting journey, but it is certainly, at this point, minor compared to many other body-gone-awry scenarios.

AVALANCHES OF ANOMALIES

Every day babies are born with anomalies. People are involved in accidents that cause trauma to their bodies. Car accidents occur. Stairs maneuvered poorly become paralyzing situations. Unexpectedly, a new disease form attaches itself to a once-healthy body, and distress descends. Diabetes, rheumatoid arthritis, a heart attack or a stroke occurs, and life shifts. A mole becomes a melanoma. Cancer cells revolt against the body. Cerebral palsy, cystic fibrosis, a blood disorder, multiple sclerosis and Down's syndrome may be familiar names, but their impact shifts bodies, as well as families and communities, into unfamiliar situations.

It is at moments like these that we all wrestle with the universal question of why pain exists, wondering why this happened to the one we know and love, or to the one we see when we look in the mirror. In some convoluted way, we wonder if it is our fault, and we allow false guilt or shame to creep in and take up residency. What, though, is the invitation from God in this life-changing event? How are we to fully be all we can be when our body is less than it could be or once was? We are left often with more questions than answers in these heart-wrenching moments. We are left also with choices: how to trust when our body feels untrustworthy and how to be the best we can be within the limitations thrust upon us.

One of the consequences of the original sin of Adam and Eve is that, as fallen people in a fallen world, every person's body will eventually suffer a physical death. The body, once made for continual union and communion with the Holy Trinity, now struggles all of the years one lives. We are born and, from that moment, we are dying. Cells die. Hair dies. We grow up, and then we die. All of us face this same reality.

For some of us, our physical bodies encounter an event that moves us further away from the wholeness of body God originally designed us all to have. As we discussed in the previous chapters, these bodies that we live in

Who do you know whose body has gone awry, and what impact has that had?

every day will one day be redeemed and be healed for eternity. For now, however, chronic illness or disability can be an unwanted companion.

PAIN'S PERPLEXITIES

We wrestled in considering how to address the issue of pain within this book. Though we all know of folks who have been healed beyond their wildest prayers, we also know others, good servants, true-hearted and faithful Christ-followers, who are left within a debilitating situation for which they have begged for deliverance, like the apostle Paul. We have no firm way of knowing what Paul's thorn in the flesh was, whether physical, emotional or spiritual. But we sense that pain haunted him, whatever form it took.

As strange as it sounds, pain is evidence that we are alive. Our inability to escape trauma in our bodies reminds us that we are all earth-bound. The choice remains, even in illness, even in disability: How can I be responsible, to the best of my abilities, limited though they are, to care for this body that transports me through this life of mine? We are mindful of the fact that some situations bring additional responsibilities upon family members. Infants, toddlers and adults with certain physical conditions must, at times, rely partially or fully on the others in their world to enable them to function through the day. Yet it is also true that, for many, there is much they can do to care for themselves.

Many writers have pondered the theological issues surrounding pain and imperfection, including Edith Schaeffer in her book *Affliction*, C. S. Lewis in *The Problem of Pain* and Philip Yancey in *Disappointment with God* and *Where Is God When It Hurts?* At the bottom line, pain gets our attention. Then we have a choice: turn to God or turn away from God. Pain, an undesired contributor to our days, contributes to our spiritual formation.

No one escapes pain's reach. It may come through temporary and minor incidents such as skinned knees, splinters or a toothache. Or it may show up and put down stakes, staying for the long haul with life-altering effects. Pain connects us to the brevity and frailness of life and the depth of God's continual presence. Pain humbles us. Pain rearranges us. Pain can lead to deeper intimacy with Christ or to a bitterness that bites the breath out of each moment. It is far easier to say we want to be made into the likeness of Christ than to actually experience that remaking, especially when pain is the mechanism involved. All of us, upon seeing pain's imprint, have the initial desire to run and hide, or run and blame. We watch Jesus pressing into pain and begging that the cup be passed on while in the same breath, Christ surrenders his will for God's own. Pain is a platform for surrender, for perseverance, for trust. It is a place to cry out for mercy.

When you encounter pain and suffering, what responses arise?

Pain is also a place where we find mercy and hope, then turn and offer hope and mercy to another. We've all experienced this. Waiting rooms, hospital corridors, cancer centers and physical therapy facilities are all places where people are suffering. Yet, even in their suffering, they are cheering one another on, offering words of encouragement and hope, even in the bleakest moments.

Pain is a breeding ground for prayer, for growth. The rich soil of pain plants us in places where we, the tender branch, cling to the vine who is Jesus, inhaling life even as death is pain's final destination. Pain and suffering carve us. As we are carved in deep places, more of our own heart and beliefs are revealed. The rawness of pain unveils who we really are. All the while Jesus is ever near, holding us close if we will let him. The surface of our life seems to vanish and we are able to see the interior of our heart more clearly. We notice areas of great strength and beauty as well as areas of weakness and woundedness. All of us have experienced moments of sorrow and sadness brought on by emotional, relational, work-related or financial pain. Yet, at times, the pain of the body we inhabit each day shouts even louder than these other types of pain.

PRESSING INTO PAIN

At the moment, among my friends and family, the causes of pain stretch from one end of the body to the other. An inventory of chronic pain, disabilities and illnesses includes a Pandora's box of symptoms declaring loudly the body's disordered state. Among the ones I count near and dear, there are many lamentations concerning the body in pain: major pain or minor aches brought on by accidents, aging, arthritis, birth trauma, cancer, diabetes, fatty liver disease, heart disease, injuries, leukemia, obesity, Parkinson's and strokes, along with the everyday incidents of colds and the flu that are perpetually being passed from one to another. Additionally, emotional responses to stress of one kind or another in our lives can make us feel sick at heart as well as sick physically. Dramatic shifts occur that alter the familiar terrain of our lives, suffocating the normalness we once breathed.

For a short season of my (Lane) life, my body encountered a muddled mess of damaged muscles and tissues. Though not a major or lingering event, pain still disrupted my sleep, my activities, my calendar, my relationships, my walk with God, my budget and my choices. Bumping into pain caused me to cry out for help. I surrendered to a new schedule of tests, of prodding and poking by a plethora of professionals: physicians, x-ray technicians and physical therapists. The prescription offered was physical therapy to rehabilitate the damaged tissues and muscles. As much as I wished for a simple pill to fix things, there wasn't one. The solution at hand was to enter a rigorous program of physical therapy, exercise to retrain muscles and rest to give my body time to recuperate. Many mornings, after a restless night of uncomfortable sleep, or lack thereof, the last thing I wanted to do was to rise early and head into more pain by going to see my well-skilled physical therapist. I longed to simply roll over and wrestle with sleep again. Yet to improve, I chose to press into the Holy Spirit's strength in the midst of my weakness to spur me on to the PT session. Even within the regimen, there were choices: choices of attitude, choices of compliance and surrender to the physical therapists' methods, choices of diligence with the at-home exercises and choices surrounding healthy eating. Choosing to simply quit would have meant accepting the pain, letting the muscles and tissues remain damaged and becoming less and less able to move and engage fully with life.

Pain is an odd thing, isn't it? Often to get to the other side of pain, we have to endure yet more pain. Sometimes the path is relatively simple. If you've ever had a charley horse, those sudden and severe cramps in your calf that always seem to happen in the middle of the night, you can relate. The only way to get that muscle to uncramp and the pain to vanish is to literally press into the pain by standing on the cramping leg or massaging it. By applying gentle pain, the deeper pain slowly relinquishes its hold. Other times, though, the path to relief is much longer: surgery, chemotherapy or radiation. In situations where pain stretches long, we wrestle. We wrestle with God about the whys and hows of such agonies. We grapple with our own physical, spiritual and emotional agony. We hurt, and we want the hurt to stop. There is no choice but to endure the physical discomfort, but what might it look like to endure it well? Pain wears many faces, and those faces cause us to struggle. We battle to hold onto hope when suffering seeks to drag us into the darkness. The problem of pain presents theological, emotional, physical and relational struggles. Agony and aches press into all arenas of our life.

Ways to counteract the sting of suffering include watching Jesus as he cares for those who hurt as well as observing Jesus as he encounters his own afflictions. Examining both his life and his relationships, we see that he understood pain as well as endured it. In what ways might we, like Christ, endure distress? Perhaps we adopt the Psalter as our prayer book when prayers don't easily come forth. For instance, we personalize and pray through Psalm 23 daily, imagining the Good Shepherd caring for us among the hurts we're enduring. Using breath prayer as our structure, we inhale and exhale Jesus' words in Matthew 11:28-29: "Come to me, all you that are weary and are carrying heavy burdens, and I will give you rest. Take my yoke upon you, and learn from me; for I am gentle and humble in heart, and you will find rest for your souls." We offer our affliction to Jesus; we stay present to Christ's presence with us, here and now. We find comfort in walking prayerfully, hand in hand with Christ, who knows our every need and remembers the depth of our hardships. By holding onto hope and being held by God's presence alongside the company of others, we find that we are not alone. Allowing others to walk with us, pray for us, serve us and encourage us in the struggles that pain brings won't end the misery, but it may make the pain more bearable.

Pain on the outside can also speak to us of pain deep within. Yet pain is not a language we are well versed in understanding. Linda, widowed six years earlier, suddenly started itching all over, sleeping poorly and encountering a nagging tiredness. Her long and happy marriage had tragically ended when her husband John died while on a mountain hike with their college-age son. Neither her therapist nor her spiritual director voiced any concern about this strange new itching and weariness that dogged her days, so far removed from her husband's death. But the minute her physician saw her, the doctor's response was swift and to the point. With wisdom laced in kindness, she said, "I'm not giving you any medicine for this, Linda. You are grieving. It is all coming out in your body." Though she had wisely done grief work right after the loss of her beloved John and had even been to seminary and become a spiritual director, Linda realized there was more restoration to be done. She needed to make peace at a new and deeper level with God, who had allowed bad things to happen. For Linda, healing came through several avenues: a GriefShare group honing in on Scripture, work with a therapist and a spiritual director, and a sweet, prayerful intimacy with Christ. A turning point occurred during a prayer walk within a labyrinth. All the way into the center of the labyrinth, she poured her anger and her laments out to God. At the center, God's response was to show her the other side of the coin, the blessings that had occurred since the tragedy. She emptied her anger. God filled her with hope. The itching vanished; energy returned. Deep within, restoration came: "God is good; he uses all for good." Through accessing the deep recesses of her heart through the Spirit's presence, pain said its goodbyes.[1]

Pain whittles me to the point of exactness. It cuts into all that I am and shows me what I'm made of spiritually, emotionally, relationally and bodily. I'm not a fan of pain, but I know it is a teacher that offers me opportunities I might not encounter otherwise: ways to deepen my intimacy with Jesus, to lean in at the end of my rope to the Holy Spirit's holding comfort and to be tenderly held as a child in the arms of my heavenly Father. Pain grounds me to earth and keeps me longing for heaven, where all is a pain-free zone.

A read through any of the Gospels assures us that Jesus cared for the sick, the paralyzed, those with short- or long-term diseases. He came and healed people's bodies: the withered hand, the shriveled legs, the ill child and the dead, brought back to life. So we know that the body, diseased or deformed, mattered to Jesus. Yet for reasons unknown, we also know that Jesus did not heal every single body during his sojourn on earth. Questions linger, as this is no easy area to tackle. But as far as possible, we are responsible to steward what we have as best we can. Figuring out how we might make the most of what often seems the worst that can happen is a challenge. It requires all of our body, mind, heart, soul and spirit as we wrestle with pain and suffering, as evidenced in daily aches and pains, minor illnesses, chronic diseases and lingering disabilities. I imagine, like Job, we usually don't receive explanations that satisfy our anger, our curiosity or our distress. Instead we receive the One who will walk through these enigmas and dilemmas with us, because we are the beloved of the Lover of our heart.

CLOSING PRAYER

Lord, it's not fair. It is just not. Some of us get more than our fair share of problems and woes, and some of us get none at all. My pain (or that of my

How do Jesus' words "I will never leave you nor forsake you" carry you in the midst of life's daily or disastrous pain?

friend, child, spouse, relative or neighbor) seems more than I can bear some days. It is easy to think of Job at times like this.

Really, God, sometimes other people can be so insensitive, so inappropriate. I do not want to be coddled like I am a child, yet there are times when I need a good cry. I do not want to be told to be good. I am trying to press in . . . but it's downright tough to do sometimes.

Lord, I also admit that at times it's hard to be on the receiving end so often. Show me how to graciously receive offers of love, yet also show me how to care well for myself and do all I can for myself.

I don't want my pain to become an excuse for a perpetual pity party.

Every day with pain (or a disability or a chronic condition) feels like I'm on a tightrope or a trapeze. I wonder: Will I fall off? Will I be caught? Do not let me give up. Let me instead give in and surrender to you, to your holding care. Give me courage when I would rather have comfort. Give me guts when I would rather retreat.

Most of all, keep my eyes on you, not my situation. Keep my heart alive and free from bitterness. And, Jesus, thank you for the cross. That reminds me that you understand pain. It also reminds me that one day you will redeem my body and it will again be full and whole and pain-free. Thank you for hope. Amen.

REFLECTION EXERCISES

1. Studies have shown that people with a spiritual life and a faith community tend to do better handling chronic conditions than those who do not. Who do you know who lives with a chronic condition? How does life with God, or lack thereof, affect their journey of daily life with the disease? What do you admire about their attitude, their body care? What makes you uncomfortable?

2. What is your perspective on suffering? Do you think suffering is the norm or the exception for Christ's followers? How might pain and suffering be teachers? Bruce Demarest in his *Seasons of the Soul: Stages of Spiritual Development* explores how such struggles and the accompanying doubts can lead us toward a depth of faith previously unknown. Edith Schaeffer also ponders troubles in her book *Affliction*. Jesus addressed some of these thoughts when he encountered the man born blind. Through study, prayer and meditation, explore your thoughts on this topic.

3. Psalm 139:13-16 talks about God forming our inward parts and knitting us together in our mother's womb. Using the holy habits of reflection and journaling, reflect on how your body

has been knit together by God. Imagine yourself in the womb. Sense God's presence with you as you were developing into the unique person you are. Think about your body's history thus far. Notice your scars and the story they tell. Notice your body's varying abilities: strengths and weaknesses. Are there aspects of your body that you struggle with? Spend some time journaling and praying about your individual creation.

9

Seasoned Well

I (Lane) am poised in a sandwiching position between several different stages of life. My first son recently became a father. My own father and mother are in their eighth and ninth decade of life. This body I inhabit shows signs of these six decades of years that have passed. Across the years, I have been a daughter, a sister, a mother, a wife, an aunt, a mother-in-law and now I am a grandparent. "Where do the years go?" we all ask as we age. A mere blink of an eye ago, I was the young woman carrying her first child. Shortly thereafter, a blessed second and third pregnancy came along. Then, a miscarriage: ectopic pregnancy leading to empty arms and a broken heart. The years tumbled onward. Three preschoolers who toddled at my knees then became school-age children. Hormones appeared and those cheerful children became, rather predictably, unpredictable teenagers. Their college and graduate school years gave way to early career adventures as young adults. While they were growing up, my parents were growing old. Just as my youngest child, a lovely young lady, finished up college, my parents encountered an avalanche of aging. My caregiving shifted from the delightfully grown children I had birthed to the parents who had birthed me. It is a familiar refrain in my circle of life these days, a fact of life: live long enough and you will grow old.

I turn the pages of my memory as I glance through old photos. I can trace the years in so many ways: hairstyles, fashions, height, weight, wrinkles gained, wisdom gained and wisdom squandered. But what does all this have to do with my body, my heart, my relationship with Christ my Lord and my relationship with others in the family of Christ?

I tend to like specific answers in Scripture. Is it right or wrong to do this particular action? It makes my life easy when God spells things out clearly for me. I imagine it makes his life easy when I actually follow what he proposes. But for most of our daily activities across most of our years, God is not that specific. Of course, Scripture does offer broad, sweeping principles aimed toward guarding our heart and keeping our mind and body in proper physical and spiritual alignment. The moment-to-moment details, however, leave much to my discretion. I can choose when to take a walk, return a phone call, e-mail a friend or eat. I can choose to listen deeply and hear God's daily invitations, but there are no scripts to follow for the story God is writing in my life.

SEASONAL CHOICES

When we begin to study the physical body and how we are to care for it across the seasons of our life, we are bamboozled a bit by the bombardment of choices at hand. Each choice, we know, precludes another choice. If I spend the hour upon rising studying the Word of God, I cannot spend that exact same hour walking the dog or working out with weights. Choices both create and negate. Saying yes here means I have said no there.

The choices I make determine the body I live within, to some degree, and the way my spiritual life matures as well. Yes, I have a height and a gene pool that predetermine some aspects of my body, but I can also make choices that shape the body and the heart I inhabit each day. Seasons of life sometimes also impact these choices. A choice that may be appropriate in one season of life shifts in another season of life. We choose as best we can as often as we can, knowing that, at times, circumstances choose for us. However, even within unexpected circumstances, we have choices.

Reflecting on our own and engaging with others to discuss the various physical and spiritual seasons is helpful for growth toward maturity. Holy habits keep our hearts connected to God's heart, and our wills aligned to God's will creates spaciousness for progression in our life's journey. Paying attention attunes us to what is really happening across the layers of our life. We notice God; we notice ourselves in response to God. We notice the interplay of our exterior and interior life.

The prayer of examen is a wonderful rhythm that can bring us toward attentiveness at any stage of life. (More details of the prayer of examen are offered within the small group guide, chapter 4, #9.) This prayerful attentiveness can even be simplified for young children, using questions more attuned to their season of life. Inviting children to notice their own heart and God's heart cultivates a thoughtfulness that enables them to move into a dialogue with God by asking questions such as: What was the best part of your day? What brought you joy? What was the hardest part of your day? When were you sad today? What do you want to thank God for? What do you want to talk to God about? With such attentiveness of heart, children and young people begin to walk the journey of a conversational, heart-to-heart delight with God.

Recreation is vital to our body and our soul. A holy resolve to create margins of simplicity, rest, play and creativity fosters rejuvenation in our multidimensional life. Though we often associate fasting with restricting our food intake, fasting can also include rearranging our busy lives to make space to enjoy life. When we are training our bodies for a race, rest days are as vital as workout days. Our hearts are no different. We need time to re-create, to rest, to simply be still and savor simple pleasures. This is not the whirlwind vacation sensation from which we return more exhausted than when we left. This is the idea of small, daily sabbaths, quieting our exterior and interior to rest and relax, to worship and enjoy the little things of the day.

Often part of what keeps our lives stretched out too thin is the upkeep involved in all that we possess, which often ends up possessing us. Simplifying what we own, what we commit to and what we care for opens hours for leisure to enjoy the quotidian moments. A night lying under the stars, an evening of reading or playing board games with friends and family, less on the calendar and more that goes to the things that are life-giving, rather than life-draining, delights and refreshes our hearts. The gift of play and recreation keep us childlike in body and heart, no matter what age we are. Laughter and attentiveness return us to the simple pleasures we once inhabited all day long as children. Enjoying life with children reminds us again that, though the body ages with each turn of the calendar, a childlike spirit still resides within each of us.

What holy habits invite you to a deeper life with God in the varying seasons of life?

FROM START TO FINISH

From the beginning, a whole and healthy child will be an active child. Just watch any gathering of infants and toddlers, then try to mimic their motions. It will wear you out. As we enter the second decade of this century, however, technology reigns. Its reign impacts our exterior and interior life. Television, computers, smartphones, electronic book readers and iPads rank high in popularity in many households, creating passive rather than active people. Many of us work long hours to make ends meet, whether as a single person, a two-parent family or a single-parent family. Overworking, overcommitted calendars and underexercising raise stress

levels for both children and adults. Likewise, the pull of busyness
and technology tugs at our spiritual maturity. Consumed with
busyness and technology, we have little time or energy left to
devote to God. We can be busy for God or busy for ourselves, but
those are false places of action. What we need is to be still enough
to engage our hearts fully with God's heart. His desire is for relationship, the long lingering of two enjoying one another. He longs
for more time with us, like a sweetheart who just wants to be with
the beloved. Yet we often become proficient in the latest technol-
ogies or rise to the top of the pack in our profession while forgetting how to go against the flow of more activities by entering
quiet stretches of long dialogues with God. Growth requires discipline and maturity. It takes time to grow. Hebrews 5:13-14 encourages us to train ourselves to discern what is good for our heart.
Proverbs 4:23 tells us to guard our heart at all costs. First Corinthians 3:1-3 reminds us to live in such a way that we are ready for
solid food, not milk only, indicating that maturity requires some
preparation and choices on our part. Busyness may look successful,
but the question is: does this engage my body and heart into a
more holy relationship with Christ himself?

Hours frittered away in front of some technological device distract us from caring well for our body and our heart. Families
often find there is little time to take an evening walk. Children
who once roamed the woods each afternoon after school now
roam the mall or the Internet instead. Teenagers are often plugged
in rather than played out. Chatting online or via text messages
ranks up there with sporting events and concerts for activities.
Once a society of participants, we are now often a society of
passive observers. "Couch potato" used to be the occupation of
only the elderly among us; now our fingers often walk more than
our bodies. Even in the midst of a recessionary season, electronic
sales soar because we falsely believe that entertainment is the way
to spend idle hours.

As we move from the busyness of starting careers and raising young families, we enter middle age. Whether through stress or sags that show evidence of a lack of diligence, or just the seasons themselves, bodies and hearts require more attentive care to maintain the flare that once came with youth's easy enthusiasm. By the time we reach old age, core strength plays a vital role in keeping us upright and strong against potential breaking of bones, which then zaps our spirits.

There are now studies that show that one's chronological age can be years older or younger than one's biological age.[1] At the church where I (Valerie) work, we just celebrated the birthday of one of our most active volunteers. Some of us were stunned to realize "Mary" was turning eighty-six. I would have said she was much younger than that, as she is still living on her own and driving. She is one of those great volunteers who does so many things that one wonders if the church will collapse when she leaves. I compare her to "Jean" who is seventy-nine. By contrast, Jean has been "old" for decades. Compared to Mary, Jean is sluggish, lacks interest and curiosity toward life, and is not very active, especially physically. Who is really the older of the two?

Much of what contributes to a person's apparent age, apart from their chronological age, is a person's attitude toward life. A person who is bored can seem older than someone who remains interested in everything, always seeking to learn something new. Some of the disparity between biological and chronological age is due to physical health and the results of lifestyle choices over a number of decades. Even if we are bedridden, we can be vibrant and alive. There are many factors that go into this disparity; some we can control while others we cannot. However, we can approach seasons of life like seasons of weather: with joy and excitement or with dread and fear. Our outlook and lifestyle choices can help us prolong the spring and summer seasons of our lives well into the time when, biologically, we are in autumn or even winter.

What do you wish someone had told you about your body at another season of life to prepare you for the one you are in?

Our body is where we live each day. Our heart, mind, soul and spirit lead us to ponder meaning within this body. Together, every component of who we are informs and impacts the other components, forming us more or less into the image of God. How we approach the years of our body and the journey of our heart during any season of life is determined not only by the physical condition our body is in but by what we think, feel and believe. To gather wisdom for our body over the seasons, let us be diligent to consider how daily choices affect future realities.

CLOSING PRAYER

Jesus, I ponder the wonder of life's seasons. Like the yearly seasons, there is something pleasurable, most of the time, about moving from one to another. At times I am ready for the change ahead, although I rarely have a true clue of what that next season has in store. Sometimes I wish I could turn the clock back, because if I knew then what I know now, how different things would have been back then. On the other hand, this change of seasons keeps me pressed up against you. I lean in and find again that your steadying hand and your lavish love surround me in this season. The challenges wear me out at times, but they also make life interesting, full of spice and full of joy.

I'm thankful for the opportunity to walk the earth, to see the sunrise, to smell fresh peaches in summer and to taste hot soup in winter. I enjoy the crunch of aspen leaves beneath my feet in fall and the icier crunch of snow in winter. I am thankful that you have saved me from myself and from others over the years, Lord.

I am thankful for precious little children. I see afresh the march of generations and aim to pray across those generations, that one season-of-lifer can tell another in a different season of life that you alone are trustworthy, faithful and true. You have seen me across many seasons, and one of these days, you will see me into the longest and best season: life forever fully in your presence. May each day prepare me for the next so that, reaching heaven, I have more blessings than regrets and more thankfulness than bitterness. May this season find me, at its end, more like you, Jesus, more like you. Amen.

REFLECTION EXERCISES

1. Journal about the place health and wellness have had in your theology about God and life. How have you functionally interacted with the question "Is physical health related to spiritual formation?" How has this shifted over the years?

2. Create a timeline of the changes of your exterior and your interior life. Indicate not only what was happening physically but also how you felt about your body at that particular age. Note what was occurring in your relationship with God at each stage of development. Did those events impact the way you felt about your body for good or for ill? Pray over your timeline, asking God to show you places that need his healing touch.

3. William Shakespeare tells of the seven ages of life in his play *As You Like It*. He starts with the infant, moves on to the schoolboy, lover and soldier, and eventually ends in a second childhood, where all reverts back to how life began: minus teeth, eyes, taste, etc. How accurate do you think his portrayal of life's seasons is? What divisions would you include if you were creating a progression of life?

10

The Next Generation

Children are prime candidates to learn discipline of any kind: mental, emotional, spiritual or physical. Since they are already so heavily engaged in learning basic skills, they more easily accept, absorb and understand intentional practices, especially ones that draw them deeper into a life of health and a closer walk with God. Teaching them to discipline their body, mind and spirit in age-appropriate ways will simply be one more way for them to understand how the world works.

By incorporating the spiritual disciplines into children's lives early on, we can give them tools for a lifetime. These holy habits will encourage them to grow in their walk with Christ and can be added to as they mature in years and faith.[1] Additionally, any adult's disciplined example, such as eating wisely, enjoying play or regularly exercising, will guide children toward living full, healthy lives. Habits, good or bad, become part of a child's life early on, and many carry over into adulthood. We learned quickly with our own children that when we sought to be healthy ourselves, it created an environment of health in the home. That milieu flooded their lives with goodness, though not perfection. Through osmosis, our children learned self-care skills, which they crafted to fit their individual personalities as they matured.

One example of children picking up bad habits with long-term consequences is the rising rate of childhood obesity. The first step in training a child in the ways of health is for the adults to seek to be healthy themselves. Children see right through the deception of "Do as I say, not as I do." If they see you exercising and eating a wholesome diet, they will be more likely to embrace that lifestyle for themselves. Even if your child or teenager is overweight, it is not too late. Instilling good eating habits and modeling regular physical activity can begin at any time. Young people who see adults making lifestyle changes for the better will be more likely to think about doing that for themselves. The Russian author Dosto-evsky once wrote, "The second half of a man's life is made up of nothing but the habits he has acquired during the first half."[2] Starting the next generation off on the right foot is important!

One simple step adults can take is to provide only healthy choices at home. If there are no unhealthy foods in your house, then both children and adults will be more likely to choose wisely. Just because the kids like it does not mean that you have to buy it. Soda pop, cookies, candy or ice cream can become things children have to purchase out of their own allowance if they want them. If the choice you offer them is between a carrot and an apple rather than a cookie and a carrot, children will naturally be making a healthy choice. If the less healthy options aren't even there, they can't be eaten. It sounds so simple, but a healthy diet begins with the grocery cart in the store. The drug education slogan "Just Say No" also applies to a host of grocery store items, including many aimed directly at children.

EDIBLE OR FOOD?

Many breakfast cereals are marketed specifically to children and placed at their eye level in the grocery store. While it may seem easier on hectic mornings to put sugary cereals out on the table and let everyone help themselves, with some advanced planning and wise shopping, you can provide quick but healthy breakfast options. Also, there are breakfast cereals on the market that contain no added sugars. Hot breakfast items, like scrambled eggs or oatmeal, can be mixed up the night before and then quickly cooked or reheated in the morning.

Sugar and chemicals make many children crankier, which only adds to the chaos of a harried morning. Refined carbohydrates cause blood sugar to rise quickly and then plummet to below pre-meal levels. Children heading off to school with that kind of breakfast will crash, that is, lose energy and mental acuity from the sugar high, negatively impacting learning. Artificially flavored and colored "fruit" snacks are another item that have little to no nutritional value. I (Valerie) remember the time a mom brought them to preschool as a snack, fully convinced they were the fruit equivalent of apple or orange slices.

Unless you are regularly shopping at a "natural" grocery store—one that focuses on organic foods—you will need to be diligent in reading ingredient lists. Our (Valerie) family was shocked into eating more healthfully when one daughter was diagnosed with allergies to food dyes, food additives and food preservatives. I learned to read labels even more carefully. When I didn't, my daughter would wake up the next morning covered in hives and struggling with severe stomach cramps. Eating organically, even when traveling, was her only option. We were amazed at the level of FDA approved dyes, preservatives and other additives prevalent in food. Yet our daughter's severe reactions showed us in dramatic ways that these are not ultimately good choices. While my daughter did eventually outgrow her allergies for the most part, our family continues to be conscious of food and my daughter pays close attention to food and exercise in caring for her body as a young adult.

Unfortunately, many things sold in grocery stores are "edible" but not necessarily "food."[3] *Edible* means that it has ingredients that won't immediately kill you if you eat them. (The long-term consequences may not be so positive.) *Food* is what God created and is what your body needs for health and longevity. Shopping the perimeters of the grocery store is good advice to follow when seeking to make changes toward a healthier diet. Most grocery stores have their produce, dairy and meat around the perimeter. The center aisles are where the canned goods and prepackaged foods are found. Those aisles are where the "edible" versus "food" issue is most prevalent.

Today there is a growing understanding among many health care professionals that "food is medicine," something our grandparents knew almost instinctively.[4] The research is beginning to show more conclusively that the food we ingest will either strengthen and heal or weaken and harm our body. Science is discovering connections between food and its impact on a child's developing body and brain which show that we really are what we eat. Poor nutrition in pregnancy can have devastating lifelong effects. The same concern is there once a child is born. Just as we don't put sand in the gas tank of a car, children can learn not to put trash in their tummies. They can begin early on to make the connection between not feeling well and having eaten a lot of junk food.

Healthy eating is more easily controlled at home. But what happens when your child is invited to a friend's house for a party or a sleepover? Generally, we believe it is best to let the child go and have a good time, even if the food they ingest is less than healthy. As they age, they will learn what it feels like to not eat well and will begin to choose the healthiest options available on their own. I (Valerie) had a friend who was very strict with what she let her children eat, even when they were guests at someone else's house. Her children became desperate to try forbidden items and began to sneak candy and other treats. One Christmas, we gave the little girl a gumball machine ornament for their tree. After it was unwrapped and the adults were talking, the child slipped away with it. We were horrified to discover she had bitten the glass top off, thinking the tiny plastic balls inside were candy. While healthy choices are always the ideal, the occasional bending of the rules keeps food from becoming a battleground. Eating well when not at home is a skill to be learned, and sometimes that learning comes from making a bad choice.

WHERE TO BEGIN

A goal might be to spend the next year transitioning your kitchen into the health center of the house. As a family, work toward having cupboards stocked with whole grains, organic fruits and vegetables, and snacks that build health rather detract from it. Start slowly. Begin to get rid of everything that has these known bad ingredients: high fructose corn syrup, preservatives and added food coloring, sugar as one of the top three ingredients, added salt and a fat content of more than 20 percent of the total calories.[5] Some foods, such as nut butters and avocados, are high in unsaturated fats, yet are nutrient powerhouses. They should be eaten in moderation, of course, but not avoided. The recommendation for the average person is that 20 to 35 percent of daily caloric intake should come from fat. Often the individual items that have a high fat content (20 percent or more) that are not nut butters include health-compromising fats or are unhealthy due to other ingredients. Experiment with more whole-wheat flour and whole-wheat pastas.[6] Foods with a very long shelf life will be suspect. Ask yourself if they would have been considered a food item one hundred years ago.[7]

Offering healthier meals and snacks can be as simple as adding in another fruit or vegetable. When preparing a meal, ask yourself, *How can I get another vegetable into this meal? Is it possible to add a bit of spinach to the spaghetti sauce or meatloaf? Can some lettuce be tucked into a sandwich? Can a cut-up apple be added to a lunch bag?* Challenge yourself to have something green with every meal, breakfast included.

Work to limit the junk food you buy. As ice cream and potato chips currently in your kitchen are eaten up, replace them with healthier choices.

What is one small change you can do this week to make your family's diet healthier?

Serve fruit and cheese for dessert. Spend most of your grocery budget in the produce, dairy, and poultry, seafood or meat sections of the store. Use the center aisle offerings judiciously; canned tomatoes are a wonderful convenience if they have not had preservatives or lots of sugar or salt added in. Think whole fruits instead of fruit juices, which have a lot of sugar that promote dental caries, especially when put in baby bottles. By starting slowly, you can make significant changes to your family's diet over the course of a year.

STRENGTHENING GOOD HABITS

Another area to watch out for is eating out of boredom or for stress release. Adults are often guilty of pacifying an unhappy child with food, teaching them early on that the answer to emotional distress is eating. Rather than using food to pacify upset children, consider making a conscious effort to spend time with them. Perhaps going for a walk, reading a book, giving them a hug or playing a game together will help teach them ways to comfort themselves apart from food. While less convenient for us in the short run, these nonfood comforts will give children a much better way to cope in the long run.

In our culture, studies increasingly suggest lack of mealtimes together as a contributor to the breakdown in families.[8] During family meals, children routinely learn manners as well as how to make conversation. When those mealtimes are infrequent or completely absent, a critical part of their socialization is missing. There is a rise in courses in table manners being taught to high school students before prom. Using a fork and napkin properly is a missing component in too many homes.

When children are allowed to play with their phone or iPad during a meal, they miss out on critical training in conversational skills. Consider making mealtimes electronic-free zones. It is not just learning the art of conversation that is being lost; children also learn how to eat proportionately and healthfully. Dr. Mehmet Oz says, "The disintegration of the family meal can be directly linked to obesity, because that's when you pass along not just the lore of the family but the taste buds of the family."[9]

Even babies benefit from human contact during their feeding times. Some are always left to fend for themselves, with a bottle propped up, so tired parents can get things done. Perhaps the reason some of us turn to food for comfort is that we are missing the full experience which eating meals together can bring. This experience comes not only from the food itself but also from the setting, atmosphere and table companions. Perhaps if we focused more on the setting, atmosphere and table companions, we might not crave food when we are feeling lonely or sad. If we live alone, frequently finding ways to eat meals with others may keep us from experiencing bouts of loneliness or sadness. When that isn't an option, we can then acknowledge the loneliness and call a friend or participate in an activity such as walking, crafting or volunteering. Food may bring a short-term sense of relief and comfort to deep emotions. However, in the long run eating to appease emotional issues will ultimately lead to weight gain or other health issues, which may add to feeling bad about life and self. Food will also not adequately address the emotional issues. Mealtimes are meant to be more than just eating. They are meant to be times of companionship and peace, filled with beauty and joy. When those elements are missing, neither the hunger of the body nor the hunger of the soul will be satisfied. This is especially important to consider when children are involved.

Someone once said they knew they had been eating out too much when their five-year-old announced at the family dinner table during a rare meal there, "This is not what I ordered!" A funny story but a sad commentary on that family. How many of us could insert our names into that story? How many of us feel that the disintegration of our family can be traced in some part to the disintegration of regular family mealtimes? How many of us eat or feed kids in the car or use mealtimes to catch up on the day's mail? Do we really know what we are eating and why?

We all know adults who, as children, learned unwise coping patterns related to food. Where might we be if we had grown up knowing not only how much God

Why do you think we approach food with so little attention to good health?

loves us but also how God values our bodies? Our bodies are such good gifts that God's Holy Spirit dwells within them. What struggles do you currently have with your body? Are their roots traceable back to childhood? If you had grown up eating as healthfully as possible and exercising regularly, would you have the same struggles? Developing good habits when they are young will set children on a good path toward growing in wisdom and in stature, and in favor with God and all the people (Luke 2:52 NLT). Children absorb our attitudes toward food, consciously and unconsciously.

INTO THE WOODS

Another issue to consider in raising healthy children is something called "Nature Deficit Disorder." This syndrome was identified by Richard Louv in his book *Last Child in the Woods*[10] and is associated with a wide range of behavioral problems in children. A lack of exposure to nature has ramifications for a child's future health, including mental, emotional, spiritual and physical. Spending time with our children outside takes time, but being in nature together is a healthy way for everyone to destress. We get our children and ourselves into trouble when we are overcommitted and then use seemingly easy things to occupy the children while racing around doing things at home. The TV seems like an easy babysitter when we are pressed for time but in the long run can lead to poor lifestyle choices.

Often when we are outside we're engaging in physical movement. Exercise doesn't have to be drudgery; it can be play: a game with a ball, a brisk walk while focusing on the fall leaves, climbing on equipment in the park, playing tag. The list of benefits from exercising keeps increasing: sleeping better at night, having more energy during the day, maintaining a healthy weight. In the long run, everyone will be healthier when less highly processed food, more rest, fewer structured activities, more outdoor physical activity and more times of face-to-face interaction are regular habits.

A FINAL CAUTION

We believe that teaching children a full range of habits is important. This includes spiritual formation habits as well as lifestyle habits. When we talk about the spiritual disciplines, fasting is one that is definitely easier to learn when started in childhood. Yet regular fasting, which speaks directly to our trust in God's provision for daily bread, requires more care when being taught to children and adolescents so that seeds of self-control, rather than an eating disorder, are sown.[11]

Introduce the concept by doing a fast from a specific food item. For example, Wednesdays could become a "no dessert day." The money saved could be collected in a small box and given to a local hunger group after several months. Substitute a time of family reading on those nights. Start with a short chapter of an interesting book, such as one from C. S. Lewis's Narnia series or an action-packed Bible story. The goal is to connect the giving up of food with the feasting on God's goodness, to make it as positive of an experience as possible. After the idea of fasting has been instilled as a regular part of children's spiritual formation, they will be more likely to accept the idea that fasting can be a help in prayer as they mature.

The discipline of fasting is one facet of the larger goal of instilling in children a desire to make healthy choices and honor God with their bodies. It can be a challenge. Issues of their body and spiritual formation will be something they'll likely wrestle with for many years, especially as they move into adolescence and the awakening of hormones. While we have to be careful not to plant or water the seeds of future eating disorders, teaching them to say no to food can also help them say no to other things as they enter the teenage years. When talking about our bodies and the role they play in our spiritual formation, it is important that as adults we always couch the language in terms of health, both physical and spiritual. We want children to have a positive sense about their bodies so that they will be more likely to care for them as they move into young adulthood.

We also want to make a solid connection in children's minds that their body is a dwelling place of the Holy Spirit. Teaching them these concepts early on can be a step toward helping them to enjoy food but not overeat. They can grow up knowing the goodness of nature and see physical exercise as a blessing, not an onerous chore. Children with those solid foundations will more likely be a healthy part of the next generation of Christ-followers and citizens of the world.

CLOSING PRAYER

God, we are here to offer mealtime graces. We come to ask your blessing for the food set before us. Even as we eat, help us think about the way you have blessed us with food. We know there are others that go hungry, even as we have our plates full.

Thank you for the sun, the rain, the soil, the seeds, the trees, the creatures, the farmers, the truckers, the grocery-store workers who all are part of what we put into out mouth at this meal.

God, thank you for this time to pause, to fill our stomachs with food and our hearts with stories of our day. Thank you for what this day has brought along, gifts of goodness even among moments that are hard.

As we eat, may we remember Jesus, the Bread of Life, the Living Water. May this moment be filled with grace to fuel us for what's next in this day. Keep us glad to be with you and thankful for your gift of food and life. Amen.

REFLECTION EXERCISES

1. If possible, plant a garden or perhaps some herbs in a small pot. Tomatoes and some other vegetables do well in small containers; it's even possible to grow strawberries in a small pot. Any way you can connect children to the earth and the source of their food will go a long way in helping them connect food with the health of their bodies.

2. Evaluate your family's eating and exercise habits. What habits are good and life-giving? Where would you like to see improvements? Slowly begin to eliminate excess activities that make healthy food preparation difficult. Replace unhealthy food choices one at a time. Substitute long periods of watching TV or surfing the Internet with being active outside. Set a new goal every two weeks or every month. Partner with a friend or another family to help and encourage each of you to slowly replace life-draining habits with life-giving ones. Change never happens quickly, but when small, measurable goals are set, transformation will happen.

3. Take your children to a farm. If that isn't possible, go to the library and find books that talk about how food is grown. Look

for ways to help them understand how cows or goats are milked twice a day. Find someone who makes cheese. See if a local bakery will do a tour. Find ways to connect children with their food sources and with the earth in general. Help them to understand the importance of rain and sunshine in the right amounts for fruit trees and vegetable crops.

11

Caring for the Planet

St. *Francis of Assisi is the embodiment* of someone who understood that there is a seamlessness to God's love and redemption for all of creation. He is known for his love of the birds and animals. One of the earliest legends about St. Francis of Assisi tells of a fierce wolf near the town of Gubbio, Italy, who was eating the village animals and inhabitants. The entire town was afraid to leave the safety of the town walls until St. Francis met with the wolf, blessed it and laid out terms of peace between the creature and the townspeople. In exchange for not attacking them, the villagers promised to feed the wolf every day, which they did until he died.[1] A lovely tale, indeed. Yet when they excavated the church at Gubbio many years later, the bones of a wolf were found under the altar.[2] The story may have a historical basis after all, and if it does, it foreshadows a reconciliation of creation as promised in Isaiah 11:6 and seldom seen since the Fall (Genesis 3).

St. Paul was aware of the promised restoration of all creation, not just humanity. He reflected on one aspect of this intimate interweaving of the various parts of creation in Romans 8:22-23:

> We know that the whole creation has been groaning in labor
> pains until now; and not only the creation, but we ourselves,

who have the first fruits of the Spirit, groan inwardly while we wait for adoption, the redemption of our bodies.

The kingdom of heaven begins here on earth; we do not have to wait for heaven. Despite the belief by some that the earth is ultimately unimportant, the incarnation of Jesus speaks against that. God so loved the world, John 3:16 tells us, that he sent his only begotten Son. The material world, creation, is important to God and will be redeemed someday along with humankind (Revelation 21:1-7). We as Christ-followers are invited to embrace and care for that creation.

In Genesis 1:28, God charges Adam and Eve to take care of, or steward, creation. That charge has never been rescinded, even after their fall into sin (Genesis 3). As a continuation of that charge, we present-day Christ-followers are to enjoy and protect the earth in all of its diversity. It is also one way to witness to our worship of the God of all creation (Genesis 2:1). Caring for the earth shows that the vision given to the prophet Isaiah by God is one we embrace as well. That vision, found in Isaiah 11:6-9, describes the time when the kingdom of God will be fully installed here on earth. Peace will reign between the animals themselves as well as between people and animals. Verse 9 promises that

> They will not hurt or destroy
>   on all my holy mountain;
> for the earth will be full of the knowledge of the LORD
> as the waters cover the sea.

This vision points to a time when life on earth will again be as it was in the Garden of Eden.

Colossians 1:15-18 is a marvelous passage about the role Christ plays in the universe. Jesus is "the image of the invisible God, the firstborn of *all* creation" (v. 15, emphasis added). He existed before all things were made and everything in the world holds together in him. "He is the head of the body, the church; . . . the firstborn from the dead" (v. 18). In short, not only did God create the world and everything in it through Jesus, all of creation is held together and redeemed by him.

Christ's burial in a garden tomb followed by his resurrection into a new spring is the beginning of the redemption of all the gardens of the earth. Through caring for the earth, we stand with Jesus in that garden place of resurrection and witness to the hope of redemption for humanity and creation alike. This reality makes stewardship of the earth part of our spiritual formation.

For example, in Matthew 6:25-34, Jesus invites us to "consider the lilies." This means that looking at, meditating on, the flowers in a field or the birds in the air helps us remember that God cares for them as well. Have you ever spent time studying a leaf, a rock, a houseplant or your pet? Considering elements of nature can expand our view of God and God's work in the world. It can also remind us that since God cares for birds and flowers, we are invited to care for them as well.

How does nature communicate the goodness of God to you?

SHOWING THE WAY

As Christ-followers, we have a reason to be at the forefront of the environmental conservation movement. Psalm 115:16 says, "The heavens are the LORD's heavens, but the earth he has given to human beings." That means that we are to care for the earth. However, it does not imply that we will all approach conservation in the same ways. Some of us will be hunters; some will be vegetarian. Some will be drawn to urban landscapes; others will be drawn to wilderness. We will not all agree on how resources should be extracted from the earth or used once they are available. However, all of us can delight in doing things that we believe will support sustainable agricultural and fishing practices, alternative energy research and healthy forest management policies. God simply asks us to delight in creation and partner with him in caring for it to the best of our ability and understanding.

If this is new information to you, there are simple ways to begin. For instance, one small step is to keep a cloth bag in your car to use when shopping. I (Valerie) remember being in Turkey on my way to one of the numerous biblical sites there. As we drove down the road, we passed a trash dump. Thousands of plastic bags had blown everywhere in the surrounding area. We gasped at the horror of the sight of all this trash blowing near Roman ruins and ruining the modern countryside. The even sadder reality is that those bags will never disintegrate and will be a part of future archaeological digs in that area centuries from now.

Consider also taking the plastic bag that your newspaper comes in to a local park where dog owners can re-use it to pick up dog waste. Recycling centers, often available in grocery stores as well as other parts of town, usually accept clean cans, bottles, cardboard, newspapers and some plastics. Create a simple bin system to collect these renewable materials at home, then incorporate dropping items off on an errand-running day.

At my (Valerie's) church, the plates, cups and utensils used at Easter breakfast are now the compostable kind. It is another way of proclaiming that Christ's resurrection from the dead is the down payment on all of creation's eventual redemption (Romans 8:19-23). It also witnesses to our belief that God created the heavens and the earth.

Is your faith community near any natural resources, bodies of water or even a small park? By raising that bit of creation up in prayer for protection, your congregation can begin to embrace a fuller view of God's love for the whole world, along with the people in it. Occasional worship services might be held in that outdoor place or it could be "adopted" for litter pick-up, tree planting or other service projects. Your larger community would then see an active witness to your belief that God so loved the world.

Sometimes the place to begin is by praying for the desire or opportunity to care for the creation, in ways that are new to you. Alone or with others, consider using this common thanksgiving prayer of the church:

> Merciful Creator, your hand is open wide to satisfy the needs of every living creature: Make me always thankful for your loving providence; and grant that remembering the account I must one day give, I may be a faithful steward of your good gifts, through Jesus Christ our Lord, who with you and the Holy Spirit lives and reigns, one God, for ever and ever. Amen.[3]

This prayer reminds us daily that we will one day give an account of how faithful we were as stewards of God's good gifts. Such attentiveness may make us more intentional in our shopping as well as in our use of nonrenewable resources.

EVERYTHING HELPS

Again, all of these attempts to care for the earth make a statement about our belief in the God of creation and our role in its care. When asked why we recycle or install energy-efficient appliances at home and at work, we can say it is because we are stewards of the creation God gave us that God continues to love. When our faith communities recycle, use compostable plates and cups for fellowship times, or seek to minimize the building's carbon footprint by lowering the heat or turning off unnecessary lights, we witness that we love the things that God loves. Having the mind of Christ, as Paul says we do in 1 Corinthians 2:16, means that we will think about the creation in the same way God does: with love and care.

In Romans 1:18-22, we are cautioned not to worship the earth.

There is a difference between honoring it as God's handiwork and worshiping Mother Nature.[4] In that passage, St. Paul notes that people who have never heard the gospel still have creation as a witness to them of the existence of God. Isn't that a marvelous thought? Creation itself witnesses for God. Psalm 19 begins:

> The heavens are telling the glory of God;
>> and the firmament proclaims his handiwork.
> Day to day pours forth speech,
>> and night to night declares knowledge.
> There is no speech, nor are there words;
>> their voice is not heard;
> yet their voice goes out through all the earth,
>> and their words to the end of the world. (vv. 1-4)

Using the discipline of meditation, we ponder the stars and planets to glimpse how God thinks. We study the seasons and notice God's faithful presence. Rocks, flowers and animals help us understand a bit of God's love of color and diversity, even God's sense of humor. Camels and giraffes are pretty funny looking, don't you think? We see how squirrels instinctively know to gather nuts for the winter and how birds know to migrate south for the winter. Salmon return to the streams they were born in to spawn; whales and hummingbirds travel hundreds of miles back and forth to nesting grounds and wintering places. How can we not stand in awe and worship? How can we who worship the Creator God not seek to care for that creation?

Another way to think of it is like this: if your friend has a car they really like and they allow you to drive it, wouldn't you take care of it? Even if it originally had a few dents and scratches, you would still bring the car back clean, full of gas and without further damage. Just as we carefully care for a friend's possessions lent to us for our use, let us care for the earth, the creation of our friend, Jesus.

A POSSIBLE MISUNDERSTANDING

Some translations of the Bible talk about subduing the earth. Unfortunately, the idea of subduing has been interpreted by some to mean exploit or abuse. In reality, subduing means that, while people have been given power over nature, that power "cannot include the license to exploit nature banefully."[5] We are to approach the physical environment in such a way that we care for it, while at the same time our lives are enhanced and enriched by it.

What is your belief about the earth and its role in Christian spiritual formation?

Also, we cannot escape this fact: what happens to creation affects us, just as we affect creation. One example is seen in some of the climate changes occurring around us. This can be a very divisive issue, with people of faith on both sides of it. All sides can agree, though, that while humans are the crown of creation, we are also dependent on that creation. As Christ-followers, we can put our efforts into caring for the earth, regardless of where we land in the discussion about its age. Like any good artist, God is still working with all of creation, making changes here and there through natural forces like erosion, volcanic eruptions and earthquakes. God invites us to be co-creators, co-artists, in the world with him, caring for what he cares for, bringing his love, blessing and healing in every place where it is needed on the planet.

John Stott, the late Church of England minister and theologian, was a lifelong birder. He wrote:

> [Psalm 104] is an early allusion to ecology, that is, to living creatures in their natural environment. . . . All creatures are dependent on their environment, and loss of habitat is the major cause of loss of species. It was Jeremiah [4:23-26] in

the seventh century BC who foretold the evils of habitat destruction. . . . If the people stubbornly maintained their refusal to repent, he cried, the Babylonian army would invade from the north and would devastate the land. . . . We would do well to reflect on Jeremiah's warning of a possible return to pre-creation chaos, darkness and devastation. One of God's creation blessings was the appearance of birds to "fly above the earth across the expanse of the sky" (Genesis 1:20); one of his judgments would be their disappearance. So let's resolve to do all we can to protect and preserve our unique God-given environment.[6]

Thoughts like this can cause anxiety. Adding guilt to an already overwhelmed life is not helpful, nor is it our intention. All of us want to simply enjoy life while seeking to walk faithfully with Jesus. At times, we want to believe that God will fix it all and if he does not, then somehow, it is "God's will." While God may intervene in miraculous ways, and already does every day, we also acknowledge the mystery that God uses men and women to do his work on earth. All of us have a vital role to play in the coming of God's kingdom.

Each person on earth is created uniquely, placed into a particular place in time, to do a part no one else can do. God is with us, but God does not take away our free will. Our response to God's call includes interacting with the people around us and the circumstances we find ourselves in. The natural world that supports and sustains human life is a continuous backdrop to our daily life. It has a role to play in our spiritual formation, just as our bodies do. For example, through the centuries, beautiful places in creation have figured heavily in the writings of people seeking to draw closer to God. The Scriptures give examples of natural phenomena responding to situations. Manna rains down from heaven and quail fly into camp at God's command to feed wandering Israelites. Water gushes from rock or stops flowing to create a dry path. Mount Sinai trembles at the presence of the Holy One, and clouds come in to cover Moses and Elijah talking with the transfigured Jesus on the mountaintop. One of the most dramatic natural responses happened when Jesus was hanging on the cross. The sky became unnaturally dark and, at his death, rocks split open as the earth shook. Creation itself was grieving the death of the Son of God.

Jesus included more ordinary examples of how creation impacts our spiritual formation as well. He likened the preaching of the Word of God to a farmer sowing seeds (Luke 8:4-15). We are invited to discern if we are rocky ground for that seed or good soil. In Luke 6:43, we are taught to discern actions by understanding that plants bear particular fruits. The implication of this parable leads us to consider whether we are a good tree bearing good fruit. Weeds, yeast, mustard seeds and calming storms are all used by Jesus to illustrate aspects of the kingdom of God. Water is blessed for baptism; bread and wine or grape juice become the body and blood of Christ in Holy Communion. Material things of the earth are transformed into symbols of God's grace and mercy. We are invited to touch, taste and see the goodness of the Lord as we seek to be better disciples of Jesus.

Thus, seeing all of creation as an integrated whole declaring God's glory and goodness assists us with a better understanding of our place within the cosmos. The larger creation helps us keep perspective on our own life and problems. It also shows us the majesty of God, reminding us on days when we are "blue" that beauty, mercy and grace always surround us. When we care for the earth, plants and animals, we show God our gratitude for that beauty, mercy and grace.

Ultimately, the stewardship of the earth is a huge issue that cannot be fully covered in this short chapter. There are widely diverse political and scientific issues that people approach with a variety of opinions, and the resources for this chapter are a drop in the bucket of what is available. The earth's stewardship involves multilayered, complex questions that must be answered by individuals who join with other members of their faith communities. Through the discipline of guidance, we seek consensus around issues that affect us locally or regionally, knowing we cannot tackle everything.

The important thing is to regularly acknowledge that we are physical beings, created in the image of God, charged with caring for the earth and its inhabitants. How each of us, individually and as members of the larger body of Christ, lives that out can add to or detract from the witness to God's creation of the world and his continuous work in it.

CLOSING PRAYER:

"The heavens are telling the glory of God; and the firmament proclaims his handiwork," declares Psalm 19:1.

How truly amazing it is, Lord, that each day I have the chance to notice your artistry as I live here on earth. In paying attention to your craftsmanship, I am led to ponder and praise you.

When I walk outdoors, I hear the wind rustling in the trees accompanied by the songbirds' music. I inhale fragrant perfume from the fir trees and the dainty flowers at their trunk. I see shades of green that shout beauty. I feel the rough places where velvet-antlered deer nuzzled the smooth white bark here in the aspen grove last fall. I notice the slender weaving of the spider's web. The tall bushes gently swaying nearby remind me of other tall bushes full of delicious blueberries, picked and eaten one summer afternoon long ago when my children were young. Such wonder, Lord, such wonder. A cathedral for my senses that I can enter any time I so choose.

God, it's interesting to think that we have fabulous museums all over the world dedicated to caring for the incredible art created by artists from across the centuries. Such museums present, preserve and restore art, offering access to such creativity to any who choose to visit. Yet every single day all of us walk in the living museum of your ingenuity, sometimes barely noticing the wonder of your creation. Worse than that, not only do we not notice the wonders, we do harm to your artwork, in ways we would never do so to a fine work of art such as a piece of sculpture, a poem or a symphony score.

Your creativity is the springboard for our own, for it is your raw materials and your modeling of splendor that lends us similar possibilities. In Exodus 31, you provided the artists with blessing and a bounty of provisions to echo your playfulness and beauty.

How am I to be part of caring for the raw materials you created? The issues seem so large, and I'm just one person. Lord, what issues can I influence? How can I offer the earth some care? What can I do this week to make some small difference? Is it through recycling or buying fruits and vegetables that are pesticide-free? Is it by investing time and energy into a community or school garden or a local CSA, supporting farmers in my community with their agricultural ventures? Is it remembering to keep cloth bags in my car when I run to the grocery store, rather than acquiring yet another plastic bag?

Your invitation is to steward well the place I live now, not just for my children, my grandchildren and myself but also as a way of living out a kingdom heart and life. Let me be care-filled and careful for creation, noticing how it teaches me of you, God, and how it draws me to you. Show me one simple way I can care for the earth today. Keep me mindful of earth, your artwork, and may I attend to it well . . . just like a museum-worthy piece of art. May my simple small acts declare with the psalmist the glory of all that you create. Amen.

REFLECTION EXERCISES

1. Read the Newberry Medal–winning book by Madeleine L'Engle, *A Wrinkle in Time*. In this story of good overcoming evil, messengers of God are not always human. Have you ever had a message from God that came through a nonhuman source?

C. S. Lewis's Chronicles of Narnia present the same concept but in a very different setting.

2. Investigate A Rocha, an international group of Christians seeking to help conserve threatened habitats around the world. Their website is www.arocha.org/int-en/index.html. They are especially interested in helping in areas where the land, plants and animals are being devastated due to extreme poverty.

3. The issue of climate change is very polarizing. Some believe it is not really happening while others are quite vocal about it. Still others believe God will take care of it and so it is not for us to worry about. How might you begin to talk about the issues this chapter raises with your faith community? Consider using Pastor Benjamin Stewart's book, *A Watered Garden: Christian Worship and Earth's Ecology*, with its discussion questions. It could be a place to begin the conversation.

Going On from Here

*F*ood for thought" has been the goal of this book. We hope you, like us, have taken the time to ponder what role the body plays in the life of the heart and its formation into Christlikeness. From ancient times, God's word has said that we are to love the Lord our God first. Deuteronomy 6:5 expands on this thought: "You shall love the LORD your God with all your heart, and with all your soul, and with all your might." There is interplay here between our interior and our exterior life.

We see this when we hear the Ten Commandments or Jesus' words in the Sermon on the Mount. Romans 12 reminds us to offer our everyday bodies as a living sacrifice that is tied up with our spiritual worship of God. In 2 Corinthians 12, Paul writes of how his body's weakness is but another way of leaning into the strength of Christ. Whatever shape or season our body is in, it is in this earthly vessel that we go through life. Our individual bodies are the temple where the Spirit of the Lord dwells and where together we are members of the church, the body of Christ, who also comes to us in the material elements of the Lord's Supper. Scripture teaches, and we believe, that this earthly body will someday be transformed into a new body to roam on a new earth. We will be held responsible for the stewardship of our body, heart, soul, spirit, time, resources and the earth on which we dwell.

MOVING FORWARD

So how do we go forward with all that we have delved into on these pages? Across the centuries, Christ's followers have sought to be wise in how they live, through engaging with Scripture, dialoguing with God in prayer, listening in silence, solitude and meditation, and through other interactions with the Holy Spirit. Ancient yet ever-renewing holy habits invite us to a more reflective life. Other ways we might become more attentive to our body and to some of the ideas in this book include meeting with a wise, Christ-centered spiritual director, creating a personal "rule of life," and enjoying the fellowship of others who long for an integrated body and heart. (For more on this, see appendix A.)

A rule of life is one way that Christians over the centuries have aimed for holiness. A series of overarching resolves, a rule of life serves as a guidepost for making choices every day. Ideally, a few specific and measurable principles guide our direction at the many forks in the road we all come to regularly. The rule encompasses all of life: physical, spiritual, emotional, intellectual, relational and occupational. How that rule gets worked out in daily life will look different for each person.

Stephen A. Macchia offers a contemporary guidebook that is helpful in creating such a rule of life. In *Crafting A Rule of Life: An Invitation to the Well-Ordered Way*, he explains that a rule is "like a trellis which offers support and guidance for a plant, helping it to grow in a certain direction," rather than a restrictive, forbidding boundary.[1] The beauty of a trellis is that it fully encourages the true fruitfulness and beauty of the plant, while keeping the tender tendrils from drooping or going astray. All of us have both exterior and interior places of great beauty and fruitfulness that often lie dormant or get trampled without a trellis for markers that guide us along. Perhaps one way to go forward in integrating body and heart is through the scaffolding that a rule of life offers.

Another attentive heart habit is the historical art of spiritual direction. This ancient relationship between spiritual director and spiritual directee alerts us to God's movements in our everyday moments. How might working with a spiritual director impact our life with Christ?

Spiritual direction is the act of paying attention to Jesus, God and the Holy Spirit. Together, spiritual director and directee meet in the presence of the Holy Spirit, to look, listen, discern, and move closer to the heart of the Holy Trinity. Within this sacred relationship, the spiritual director encourages the directee to develop a deeper life with Christ. Just as a personal trainer at a gym helps a person's body stretch and grow, a spiritual director helps a person's heart and soul stretch and grow in areas of life with Christ.[2]

Spiritual direction is not a counseling, discipling, coaching or mentoring relationship but is, rather, a prayerful journeying together toward noticing God's presence across all aspects of one's interior and exterior life. As a spiritual director, I (Lane) describe it this way:

Like a driver changing lanes, there are blind spots of which to be aware. The spiritual director's role, like mirrors, maps, and traffic signals, enables you to notice and traverse the terrain of your own heart and soul, as you journey with Jesus.[3]

A spiritual director's role is to pray with and for you, be attentive with you through asking questions that lead you deeper into your own heart and God's, and may include suggesting Scripture, holy habits and various types of prayer so you can discern the Holy Spirit's daily work and invitations in your life.

All of life matters to God. As we intentionally journey deeper with God, the body begins to be more obvious to matters of our heart and daily life. One of my directees recently commented that

> by being in spiritual direction, I have become more aware of
> what my body is telling me and paying attention to that. I am
> sensing when I am tense or tired, instead of just passing it off
> or not even noticing it like before, I slow down and question it
> to see if I need to learn from what it is telling me. I think I have
> become more aware of asking to see Jesus in my now moments,
> and that involves my body. As I am becoming more attuned to
> that, I am sensing an excitement in myself as I invite Jesus into
> places that I wasn't even aware I had been keeping him out of.
> . . . This is an area that I feel I can stretch and grow in.[4]

With my own spiritual director, I explore hints my body sends that act as exclamation points of ah-ha moments or flashing yellow lights, indicating oh-no moments. When my body speaks, my spiritual director helps me listen to God's voice in the mix of my exterior and interior life.

When we are intentional, we pay attention. We seek to keep our hearts open and vulnerable to God's heart, moving at the behest of his will and the Spirit's nudges. We seek to be connected to our body, our heart, our environment, our relationships and all aspects of our particular, unique life as we walk with God. Intentionality leads to integration, a more unified whole of all the parts of our existence. When we take steps to be more intentional, we do so in ways that are specific and measurable. It is a way we can see how we are making progress away from unholy habits that we struggle with regularly. These words—*intentional, specific* and *measurable*—signify the rule of life we had when writing this book. In your life, they are meant to bring a greater degree of physical and spiritual health.

Is physical health related to spiritual formation? Yes, we believe so. The body and heart impact each other regularly and significantly. The deep intimacy of a relationship with Christ's own heart, a sound theology of who God is, and a solid understanding and living out of our own identity in Christ is foundational as we move forward in transformation. Staying present to Jesus' heart, we stay present to our own heart. Change comes as we assess and declare our priorities, then begin to order our days in such a way that all aspects of our life—body, soul, heart, spirit, will and mind—unite more fully within us, moving us toward wholeness and holiness, aligned well with the will of God. May holy resolve and joyful attentiveness be intertwined throughout the entirety of our life in the body within the body of Christ.

CLOSING PRAYER

Change. It's part of life. It's part of transformation. It's good and exciting; it's hard and scary.

Change. It's as inevitable as the fact that the sun will rise tomorrow and as unpredictable as the wind that is sure to blow.

Change. Easier said than done. Easier to wax eloquently about than to move forward into.

Change. Lord, I desire change: change to become more like you, Jesus. Change to become more concerned about my own health of body and heart and the health of my brothers and sisters who make up this family you call your beloved Bride. Change to care well for the earth while not following the culture that makes idols everywhere and knows little about true worship.

I am to worship you in spirit and in truth. That will only happen by your Spirit, by your heart, and by your truth infusing me, so that the aroma of my life is the scent of grace, love, mercy, holy resolve, stewardship and, most of all, you. Amen.

Acknowledgments

It is one thing to have an idea for a book. It is another to see that idea come to fruition. To Cindy Bunch and the InterVarsity Press staff, thank you for welcoming our idea and shepherding it forward. God uses your gifts and talents in powerful and diverse ways.

FROM VALERIE

Books come out of the fullness of our lives. The coalescence of ideas on and experiences with spiritual formation, theology and physical health have come from a variety of sources over many years. First of all, I owe my husband a big thank-you. John has lived each of my books with me. Through the good and the hard times of writing, he always shows patience and grace-filled support. Over many years, his theology and ponderings on the kingdom of God have sunk deeply into my mind and heart. It is hard to separate out his ideas from mine at times, and so his fingerprints sprinkled throughout this book need to be acknowledged and thanked.

I want to thank Lane, my coauthor, through whom God worked as iron sharpens iron. She brought different gifts to this project than what I have. It made for a richer end-product and I am a better person for it as well.

Richard Foster and Renovaré have changed my life. Throughout the writing, many Renovaré staff and board members have been a big encouragement. Thank you.

My students in the Master of Spiritual Formation and Leadership program (MSFL) at Spring Arbor University were my test case with this idea that physical well-being and spiritual formation are interwoven. I have learned a lot from them over the years and owe them a debt of gratitude.

Barb Steiner has been my spiritual companion and friend for years. Her gift of orderly thinking coupled with her unconditional love has helped me clarify my thoughts during writing and in my life in general. Thank you for holding my hand when the waters were rough.

The staff at Trinity Lutheran Church, Boulder, Colorado, has also been very supportive during this time of writing. They often asked how the book was coming along and let me slip away at times to focus on it. I am blessed to work with people who love God and love the church in its local manifestation.

God has filled my life with a variety of people with a diversity of thoughts, opinions and beliefs. Deep thanks to you all, too numerous to name. Your enthusiastic support and willingness to postpone social engagements during times of intense writing helped immensely. Oftentimes, you had no idea that God was speaking to me through you.

And finally, but really at the beginning surrounding all: To God be all the glory, now and forever, unto the ages of ages. Amen.

FROM LANE

All that is good herein comes from your good heart, God. Your presence gifts me with wordsmithing and, in turn, Word-smiths me. You use it all to write your big story. May all the glory be yours, knowing any flaws herein are mine alone.

Ohana, you bring such joy to my heart by who you each uniquely are. You remind me who and Whose I am. Robert, among our walks, talks, playfulness, moves, waitings and even in the Waldo Fire evacuation, you've been for me every step of the writing way. Who'd have thought we'd be sharing these good dreams coming alive together?

Deep gladness surges forth for you who cheered, reminded and listened as I wrestled and wrote. I-team, you had my back and you had my heart. I'm honored to be among your shimmering wonder. Patty and St. Ignatius, blessed be your spiritual direction into spacious surrender with Jesus. John S., I'm staying present. Gloria, your untender mercy rejuvenates. Sue R. and Stasi Rose, when my heart dipped down, your beauty sent me soaring. Accolades to Anne, Cheryl F., Kellye, Janis, Lynne, Susan and Wendy for profound questions among found moments. Cheryl N., cheers for cascading laughter always. Paul and Marjorie, your generous hearts offered beauty and quiet at Denver Seminary. Jim and Margaret, what graciousness to nomadic boomerangs. RH, the wooing beauty and winsome glory of Sacred Romance invited healing and freedom. Hurray to CSAs, community, church and school gardens: you grow hope in your green garden plots. Valerie, thank you for mentoring me through my first publication. Such poetry of presence, people, place and ponderings infuses my life. A tip of the heart to the many unnamed yet not forgotten who've also been some part of this writing rhythm. Thanks be to God for all that is and was and is to be.

Holy Habits for the Whole Body

The well-being of our souls and our bodies is strengthened through the use of various spiritual disciplines. We often think of the spiritual disciplines as relating only to heart and soul; however they also involve our body. Spiritual formation for Christ-followers is anything that forms us into more Christlikeness. The goal is to make this training intentional. Trevor Hudson writes:

> These spiritual disciplines are not a way of earning salvation. They do not accumulate for us any heavenly merit or spiritual capital. Our acceptance by God, as we are, rests on grace alone. However, there is nothing automatic about the maturing of our spiritual lives. We become more like Jesus only as we make certain purposeful responses to the freely given grace of God. *In addition to our habitual reliance on Christ, the purposeful, strategic use of our bodies represents our essential part in the transformation process.* Participation keeps our feet walking along the Pilgrim Way, opens our hearts to receive the divine love, and positions us before God so that the Holy Spirit can work within us.[1]

Here are some working definitions of the classic spiritual disciplines as outlined by Richard Foster in his groundbreaking book *Celebration of Discipline*. We have added a physical perspective to the definitions to help illustrate the interrelatedness of our souls and our bodies in spiritual formation.

- *The discipline of meditation:* Here we learn to soak in God's Word, like a tea bag in hot water. This discipline is about slowing down, using silence and concentration to savor the Bible, the goodness of God in creation, art or music—anything that fills our mind with the truths of God is worthy of our attention. Because we eventually take on the properties of the object of our focus, the goal is to fill our minds as much as possible with God and God's work in the world. "We are what we repeatedly do [focus on]. Excellence, therefore, is not an act but a habit," as Dennis Bakke reminds us.[2] Meditation can be done sitting in a chair, going about the tasks of the day or walking in nature; it is an intentional focusing of our whole being on the things of God, noticing that God is at work everywhere.

- *The discipline of prayer:* Prayer is both a discipline and a spontaneous conversation with God throughout the day. It is a discipline when we pray at set times on a regular basis, even when it is not feelings- or situation-dependent. We stop what we are doing and pray, often using prewritten prayers like the Lord's Prayer to "prime the pump." That style of prayer can then be blended into spontaneous prayer for people, places and events we are aware of. There are various bodily postures we can use, which we explored in chapter 3, such as kneeling, standing, hands open or raised, or prostration on the floor.

- *The discipline of fasting:* With our bodies, we fast for the specific purpose of focusing more clearly on God's word to us concerning a general or a specific situation. This is one of the best examples of the body/spirit connection, because in denying our bodies food, we seek to draw closer to God in our souls. We can also fast from activities, using the time for prayer or Scripture reading. This discipline works best if we balance what we are giving up with what we are adding in, such as fasting from lunch and doing Bible study or taking a prayer walk.

- *The discipline of study:* While closely related to the discipline of meditation, here we seek to memorize Scripture, study the Bible through the use of commentaries, and engage with classic and modern Christian writers. We educate ourselves more specifically about the things of God, even "considering the lilies" (Matthew 6:28) as we walk in God's creation. Many times the disciplines flow into and out of each other, as with study flowing into meditation and prayer. All of them inform, correct and balance each other, much like a balanced food diet includes servings from all the food groups. In training or disciplining our minds, we find that changes in our actions become possible as well.

- *The discipline of simplicity:* This deals with our calendars, our checkbooks and our conversations. We learn to keep a level of material possessions appropriate to the season of life we are in, and to engage in conversations and activities that leave us rested. This in turn allows us to spend more time with God and others. Here again, we see the body/mind connection. If we have room to breathe in our lives, we are more likely to be rested and re- laxed. Overcommitting to activities or spending beyond our fi- nancial means stresses our body and our spirit. God gave us a twenty-four-hour day. We assume that God felt that was ade- quate to do all that he created us to do.

- *The discipline of solitude:* This includes silence, but more impor- tantly, we learn to quiet our minds and our bodies so that God can speak to us. This discipline is meant to be "portable" so that we always have a deep well operating in the center of our souls from which we can draw calm words of wisdom. Physically removing ourselves from all other distractions helps us listen better for the still, small voice of God.

• *The discipline of submission:* This is where we learn the freedom of not always having our own way. At times throughout history, the idea of submission has been horribly abused. Therefore, the first thing we learn in this discipline is Whose we are and who we are. This leads to a better understanding of what godly authority is and is not. This discipline is also very helpful for making body/mind connections. When we discipline ourselves in one area of life, it can overflow into other areas of life.

• *The discipline of service:* The exercises in this discipline teach us the difference between godly service and self-righteous service. The latter is often a thin veneer for seeking attention and applause, while godly service happens anywhere, anytime, with anyone. Service often involves doing a physical task for someone; the attitude of our hearts will be revealed loud and clear through our bodies. For example, if we are glad to be serving, our body will be relaxed. If we dislike what we are doing, that tension will be expressed in our face and in the possible jerkiness of our movements.

• *The discipline of confession:* Here we learn that in confessing our sins, we find freedom from guilt and move toward deeper healing. We use our mouths to speak the words of our hearts. Some faith communities have regular times for private confession to a clergyperson; others encourage sharing with a spiritual director or mentor. The laying on of hands or a hug can add a physical dimension to the experience. Sometimes the physical act of saying our confession out loud helps us hear God's voice through another person saying words of forgiveness and healing. Writing it out can also be helpful.

• *The discipline of worship:* This becomes a discipline through the regular commitment to gathering with a Christ-centered faith community. Like the discipline of prayer, it too is not feelings-

or situation-dependent. The act of physically being with others to worship God involves our whole being—body, mind and spirit—as we sing, stand, kneel, sit and clap.

- *The discipline of guidance:* This discipline can apply to individuals or to groups large and small as we seek to follow Christ's call, individually and corporately. Through prayer, listening for God's voice (meditation), fasting, searching the Scriptures, seeking the counsel of others, using the mind that God gave us to reason with and even "gut feelings," we seek to hear God's will for ourselves or for our faith communities.

- *The discipline of celebration:* Based on Philippians 4, this is the call to think on those things which are true, right and good; that is, the things of God. We learn to give thanks *in* all circumstances, though not necessarily *for* all circumstances. Rejoicing can involve our whole body: dancing, leaping, clapping, laughing, smiling and playing. The body is clearly a mirror of the soul in this discipline.

These holy habits, spiritual disciplines, come from Scripture as well as from centuries of Jewish and Christian thinking and practice. You will find them woven in throughout the book.

The Bible and
the Body

The Bible has much to say about the body: our physical body; the body of Christ, the church; and the body of Christ as the Lord's Supper. We read in Romans 12:1, "I appeal to you therefore, brothers and sisters, by the mercies of God, to present your bodies as a living sacrifice, holy and acceptable to God, which is your spiritual worship." This verse sums up, in many ways, the integration of the Bible's view of our body and soul/spirit working together in harmony to love and serve God. The discussion of other passages below is not exhaustive but will serve as a beginning for those who wish to pursue this idea further.

God gave ancient Israel numerous laws that deal with the body: what happens if someone touches a dead body (Numbers 6:11), what happens to someone who contracts leprosy (Leviticus 13:13), the kind of underwear priests are supposed to wear (Leviticus 6:10), what to eat and what not to eat (see Leviticus 11 and Deuteronomy 14). According to God, what ancient Israel ate and wore and what they did with or to their bodies had an impact on their prayer and worship life. Jesus fulfilled the law, but is any of it still valid for Christ-followers in the twenty-first century?

The book of Job and Isaiah 53 both describe the impact of physical suffering on the way people view God. By contrast, the Song of Solomon describes in its poetry the erotic use of the body. Some see it as a metaphor for Christ, the bridegroom, and his relationship to his bride, the church. Suffering and sex are two topics we struggle with in modern society. How might we claim a biblical understanding of both from these passages?

The Psalms and the Wisdom Literature books of Proverbs and Ecclesiastes also talk frequently about the body. Psalm 16:9 shows the interconnectedness of a heart that is glad, a soul that is rejoicing and a body that is resting secure. Psalm 139:13-16 notes the time and care God took in creating a specific body for us, even laying out the number of its days. Peter, in his sermon on Pentecost (Acts 2:26), quotes the part of Psalm 16 that promises "my body also will live in hope" (NIV). In doing so, he proclaims that the resurrection of the dead, which will happen at the end of time, will include our bodies as well as our souls, just as it did for Jesus after his crucifixion.

Proverbs 16:24 connects pleasant words with sweetness in the soul and health in the body. Have you ever felt physically ill after an argument with someone? Then you can attest to the truth of that connection. The Bible always sees a person as an integrated whole of body, heart, mind and spirit.

Proverbs 3:8 says that trust in God will be healing for our flesh and refreshment for our bodies. Proverbs 4:22 notes that those same things will happen when we walk in the paths of righteousness and wisdom, and Proverbs 14:30 notes, "A tranquil mind gives life to the flesh, but passion makes the bones rot." Those of us who have been "in a stew" over something know the truth of that statement.

Ecclesiastes 12:12 points out that too much study can weary the body, to which anyone studying for a major test can say "Amen." Somehow struggling to fill the mind with information tires the body. Why might that be?

In an unusual passage, Daniel 4:33 describes how God changed Nebuchadnezzar into a donkey as punishment for pride and arrogance. Nebuchadnezzar would not change his heart so God changed his body. Could some of our physical sufferings be God's way of trying to get our attention when we have not paid attention to the nudging of his Spirit in our heart?

In the Sermon on the Mount, Jesus says it is better to lose a body part than to be cast into hell (Matthew 5:29-30). He also describes the eye as the lamp of the body (Luke 11:34). Our bodies carry our souls; if we are polluting one, the other is affected.

Jesus referred to his physical body as a temple (John 2:21), in contrast to the temple that was in Jerusalem at that time. Throughout the Passion story, written about in all four Gospels, we see Jesus suffer deeply in body, heart, mind, soul and spirit. We cannot imagine the physical pain he endured from the beatings, whippings and nails being driven through his hands and feet. What may be even more difficult is to try to imagine the psychological or emotional pain he suffered. I (Valerie) once heard a sermon preached on Luke 23:44. The verse describes how during Jesus' crucifixion darkness "came over the whole land" from noon until 3 p.m. The preacher said that the darkness symbolized both the agony of spirit Jesus was suffering as well as the physical torture he endured. Whether or not that is true, we can safely assume that Jesus struggled fully as a human being on the cross, even to the point of feeling utterly abandoned by God (Mark 15:34).

In Romans 6:12, Paul talks of the body being an important part of the sanctification process: "Therefore, do not let sin exercise dominion in your mortal bodies, to make you obey their passions." In chapter 7, he goes on to say that being a Christ-follower is like being in a marriage relationship; just as adultery may destroy a marriage, so using our bodies for "sinful passions" may destroy our walk with God. We cannot be one way in church and another way in the rest of our life.

In Romans 12:4, Paul describes physical body parts, using them as a metaphor for the body of Christ. He uses the same analogy in 1 Corinthians 12 when talking about spiritual gifts. In Ephesians 3:6 and Colossians 1:18, Paul again uses the image of a human body for the body of Christ, the church universal. In each of these cases, the diversity within the human body is used to describe the vast diversity found in the body of Christ.

First Corinthians 6:19-20 commands us to honor God with our body because it is a temple of the Holy Spirit, echoing Jesus' statement above. We are not to sin against our body, in this case through sexual immorality. We are to train the body so it carries the soul well. In 1 Corinthians 9:24-27, Paul compares himself to a boxer who trains his body. Paul says he trains intentionally because a well-trained body will aid his preaching to others and will enable him to "get the prize" of eternal life. St. Francis of Assisi called his body "Brother Ass," meaning it was the beast of burden that carried his soul. Just as we care for a donkey, horse or camel so that it is helpful to our work, we care for our own physical body so that it is helpful to the work God has given each of us to do here on earth. By contrast, one does not let a beast of burden "call the shots," but trains it to follow commands so that it is an aid in the work.

First Corinthians 11:27-29 discusses the mystery of the bread and the wine of the Eucharist, or the Lord's Supper, becoming the body and blood of Christ. In 1 Corinthians 11:30, Paul talks about some who have died because they sinned against the body and blood of Christ through a misuse of the Lord's Supper, taking it into their own bodies inappropriately. Earlier in the letter to the Corinthians he writes, "For all who eat and drink without discerning the body, eat and drink judgment against themselves" (1 Corinthians 11:29). This points to a direct connection between our body and our soul, a connection that hearkens back to the dietary laws of Leviticus (see, for example, Leviticus 11:1-23).

In 1 Corinthians 15:12-44, Paul gives a marvelous description of what happens after death. In the resurrection we will have a body, just as Jesus did. Yet it will be different enough from what we have now, as Jesus was not immediately recognized by Mary Magdalene at the tomb or by the disciples on the road to Emmaus. In the Gospel accounts where the resurrected Christ is present, Jesus astounds people by suddenly appearing or disappearing. Yet he can eat fish and is recognized as being himself after people recover from their shock at his appearance.

Second Corinthians 4:10 says, "We always carry around in our body the death of Jesus, so that the life of Jesus may also be revealed in our body" (NIV). It is a mystery that through the sacrament of baptism, we die and rise again into a new life in Christ, a life that will find its completion at death. In Galatians 6:17 Paul claims that he bears the marks of Jesus on his body. One interpretation of these marks is that they are in some way physical.

The question of this book has been "Is physical health related to spiritual formation?" Philippians 1:20 answers affirmatively when it says: "It is my eager expectation and hope that I will not be put to shame in any way, but that by my speaking with all boldness, Christ will be exalted now as always *in my body*, whether by life or by death" (emphasis added). Paul assumes that physically with our body, as well as with our words and actions, we glorify or dishonor God.

The blessing Paul gives to the Thessalonians (1 Thessalonians 5:23) is that their spirit, soul *and* body would be kept sound, that is, healthy and blameless for the coming of Christ in glory. Our physical bodies, as well as all of the material creation, are not going to be thrown out like some bit of trash. They will be transformed as part of the new heaven and earth. The idea that there will be a new earth as well as heaven is often neglected in the thinking of many Christians. What does this mean in terms of caring for the earth here and now?

Peter writes, "Since therefore Christ suffered in the flesh, arm yourselves also with the same intention (for whoever has suffered in the flesh has finished with sin), so as to live for the rest of your earthly life no longer by human desires but by the will of God" (1 Peter 4:1-2). Using graphic physical terms, Peter then goes on to describe the kind of activities these Christ-followers formerly participated in as pagans: debauchery, lust, drunkenness, orgies, carousing and detestable idolatry. As Christians, holiness and righteousness apply to all areas of our life: our speech, interaction with others and the way we treat our body. Sometimes it seems that those who claim to follow Christ don't believe that their physical actions and professed beliefs are meant to be congruent.

Throughout the Bible, the body is an important part of who we are as people created in the image of God. God created Adam from the earth. He physically took Israel from bondage in Egypt to the Promised Land, using physical plagues to win their release from Pharaoh. Along the way, God showed his people practical ways to live their daily life well. Giving them water in the desert and manna to eat in the wilderness, God provided for their physical bodies, in addition to giving them directives for worship and interacting with each other.

God sent Jesus in the flesh to show us the Father's face. Jesus was born of Mary in the way all human beings come into the world. Jesus died but was raised again; we who trust in him can count on that happening to us too. When we become Christ-followers, it is not a mere assent to some list of beliefs; it is meant to be a radical shift in the way we live. We may need to change occupations or sever relationships. Lifestyle choices may need to be re-examined.

Following Christ involves all aspects of who we are: body, mind, heart, soul, emotions, thoughts, words and deeds. Our spiritual transformation happens in a real body, living a concrete daily life. The two are intertwined, for as the Bible shows consistently, paying attention to both body and soul in this life has implications for the life to come.

Appendix C

Resources

For each chapter, we list three to five resources that can be used to explore the chapter's themes more fully.

Chapter 1: Jesus Has a Body

Eldredge, John. *Beautiful Outlaw: Experiencing the Playful, Disruptive, Extravagant Personality of Jesus.* New York: FaithWords, 2011.

Issler, Klaus. "Learning from Jesus to Live in the Manner Jesus Would If He Were I: Biblical Grounding for Willard's Proposal Regarding Jesus' Humanity." *Journal of Spiritual Formation & Soul Care* 3, no. 2 (Fall 2010): 155-80.

Smith, James Bryan. *The Good and Beautiful Life: Putting on the Character of Christ.* Downers Grove, IL: InterVarsity Press, 2010.

Chapter 2: Bodies Within the Body

Bonhoeffer, Dietrich. *Life Together.* New York: Harper & Row, 1954.

Schaeffer, Edith. *L'Abri.* Wheaton, IL: Tyndale House, 1969.

Smith, James Bryan. *The Good and Beautiful Community: Following the Spirit, Extending Grace, Demonstrating Love.* Downers Grove, IL: InterVarsity Press, 2010.

Chapter 3: Our Body in Worship

Boa, Kenneth. *Conformed to His Image: Biblical and Practical Approaches to Spiritual Formation.* Grand Rapids: Zondervan, 2001.

Foster, Richard J. *Streams of Living Water: Celebrating the Great Traditions of the Christian Faith*. New York: HarperOne, 2001.

Hall, Christopher A. *Worshiping with the Church Fathers*. Downers Grove, IL: InterVarsity Press, 2009.

Thomas, Gary. *Sacred Pathways*. Grand Rapids: Zondervan, 1996.

Chapter 4: Toward a Balanced Lifestyle

Challum, Jack. *Stop Prediabetes Now: The Ultimate Plan to Lose Weight and Prevent Diabetes*. Hoboken, NJ: John Wiley & Sons, 2007.

Hanley, Jesse Lynn, M.C., and Nancy Deville. *Tired of Being Tired*. New York: Berkley Books, 2001.

Hensrud, Donald, M.D. *The Mayo Clinic Diet*. Intercourse, PA: Good Books, 2010.

Hudson, Trevor. *One Day at a Time: Discovering the Freedom of 12-Step Spirituality*. Nashville: Upper Room Books, 2007.

Chapter 5: A Theology of Food

Kingsolver, Barbara, with Steven L. Hopp and Camille Kingsolver. *Animal, Vegetable, Miracle: A Year of Food Life*. New York: Harper Perennial, 2007.

Pollan, Michael. *Food Rules: An Eater's Manual*. New York: Penguin, 2009.

Showalter, Carol, with Maggie Davis. *Your Whole Life: The 3D Plan for Eating Right, Living Well, Loving God*. Brewster, MA: Paraclete Press, 2007.

Sider, Ronald J. *Rich Christians in an Age of Hunger*. Dallas: Word Publishing, 1997.

Wittenberg, Margaret M. *New Good Food: Shoppers Pocket Guide to Organic, Sustainable, and Seasonal Whole Foods*. Berkeley, CA: Ten Speed Press, 2008.

Chapter 6: Questioning Cultural Messages

Bauer, Susan Wise. *The Well-Educated Mind: A Guide to the Classical Education You Never Had*. New York: W. W. Norton, 2003.

Elsheimer, Janice. *The Creative Call: An Artist's Response to the Way of the Spirit*. Colorado Springs: Shaw Books, 2001.

Kapikian, Catherine. *Art in Service of the Sacred*. Edited by Kathy Black. Nashville: Abingdon, 2006.

Roller, Julia L. *25 Books Every Christian Should Read*. New York: HarperOne, 2011.

Wright, Craig. *The Maze and the Warrior: Symbols in Architecture, Theology, and Music.* Cambridge, MA: Harvard University Press, 2004.

Chapter 7: Extremes Examined

Johnson, Jan. *Surrendering Hunger: 365 Devotions for Wholeness.* Brewster, MA: Paraclete Press, 2009.

May, Gerald G., M.D. *Addiction & Grace: Love and Spirituality in the Healing of Addictions.* San Francisco: HarperSanFrancisco, 1988.

Moore, Beth. *Breaking Free: Making Liberty in Christ a Reality in Life.* Nashville: Broadman & Holman, 2000.

Scazzero, Peter. *Emotionally Healthy Spirituality: Unleash a Revolution in Your Life in Christ.* Nashville: Thomas Nelson, 2006.

Swenson, Richard A., M.D. *Margin: Restoring Emotional, Physical, Financial and Time Reserves to Overloaded Lives.* Colorado Springs: NavPress, 2004.

Chapter 8: The Body Gone Awry

Demarest, Bruce. *Seasons of the Soul: Stages of Spiritual Development.* Downers Grove, IL: InterVarsity Press, 2009.

Lewis, C. S. *The Problem of Pain.* San Francisco: HarperSanFrancisco, 2001.

Schaeffer, Edith. *Affliction.* Grand Rapids: Baker Books, 1978.

Yancey, Philip. *Disappointment with God.* Grand Rapids: Zondervan, 1988.

———. *Where Is God When It Hurts?* Grand Rapids: Zondervan, 1977.

Chapter 9: Seasoned Well

Allender, Dan B. *To Be Told: Know Your Story, Shape Your Life.* Colorado Springs: WaterBrook Press, 2005.

Eldredge, John. *Fathered by God.* Nashville: Thomas Nelson, 2009.

Eldredge, John and Stasi. *Captivating: Unveiling the Mystery of a Woman's Soul.* Nashville: Thomas Nelson, 2011.

Feldmeier, Peter. *The Developing Christian: Spiritual Growth Through the Life Cycle.* Mahwah, NJ: Paulist Press, 2007.

Griffin, Emilie. *Souls in Full Sail: A Christian Spirituality for the Later Years.* Downers Grove, IL: InterVarsity Press, 2012.

Chapter 10: The Next Generation

Bass, Dorothy C., and Don C. Richter, eds. *Way to Live: Christian Practices for Teens.* Nashville: Upper Room, 2002.

Brizee, Lori S., M.S., R.D., C.S.P., with Sue Schumann Warner. *Healthy*

Choices, Healthy Children: A Guide to Raising Fit, Happy Kids. Brewster, MA: Paraclete Press, 2011.

Hess, Valerie E., and Marti Watson Garlett. *Habits of a Child's Heart: Raising Your Kids with the Spiritual Disciplines.* Colorado Springs: NavPress, 2004.

Physicians Committee for Responsible Medicine, with Amy Lanou. *Healthy Eating for Life for Children.* Hoboken, NJ: Wiley, 2002.

Reisser, Paul C., M.D. *Family Health, Nutrition & Fitness.* Carol Stream, IL: Tyndale House, 2006.

Chapter 11: Caring for the Planet

McMinn, Lisa Graham, and Megan Anna Neff. *Walking Gently on the Earth: Making Faithful Choices About Food, Energy, Shelter and More.* Downers Grove, IL: InterVarsity Press, 2010.

Newman, Nell, with Joseph D'Agnese. *The Newman's Own Organics Guide to a Good Life: Simple Measures That Benefit You and the Place You Live.* New York: Villard, 2003.

Shaw, Luci. *The Green Earth: Poems of Creation.* Grand Rapids: Eerdmans, 2002.

Stewart, Benjamin M. *A Watered Garden: Christian Worship and Earth's Ecology.* Minneapolis: Augsburg Fortress, 2011.

Stott, John. *The Birds, Our Teachers: Biblical Lessons from a Lifelong Bird-Watcher.* Peabody, MA: Hendrickson, 2000/2007.

Conclusion: Going On from Here

Baker, Howard. *Soul Keeping: Ancient Paths of Spiritual Direction.* Colorado Springs: NavPress, 1998.

Evangelical Spiritual Directors Association. www.ecswisdom.org/index.php/esda.

Hyatt, Michael. *Creating Your Personal Life Plan: A Step-by-Step Guide for Designing the Life You've Always Wanted.* Franklin, TN: n.p., 2011. Available online at www.michaelhyatt.com.

Macchia, Stephen A. *Crafting a Rule of Life: An Invitation to the Well-Ordered Way.* Downers Grove, IL: InterVarsity Press, 2012.

Willard, Dallas. *The Great Omission: Reclaiming Jesus's Essential Teachings on Discipleship.* New York: HarperOne, 2006.

Appendix D

Small Group Study Guide

S*piritual formation is about being* transformed into the likeness of Christ as spoken of in 2 Corinthians 3:18 and Colossians 3:1-11. Such change takes place at the intersection of a heart engaged with God's own heart. Much information has been offered within this book. If all you do is read the book, you will have garnered new data, which may shift some of your thoughts. For deeper transformation to occur, however, the data must become part of daily life through being actively engaged in response to your readings.

For all of us, change is a bit unsettling. That's why we need the body of Christ around us, cheering us on, helping us unearth tangled roots that trip us up and then curtail and prevent growth. Through relationships with people who know, trust and love us, we find a safe place to experiment with new questions and actions that combat our comfortable ways. As you've read the chapters, they've each had exercises designed to help you as an individual engage with God. This small group study guide invites you to go forward with others in this adventure of transformation.

When your small group meets, begin by first reflecting on what individual reflection exercises you've each entered into since the last gathering. The questions posed within each chapter are also possible springboards for discussion. Then progress forward, using the small group guide to deepen the conversation and spur one another on. The study guide is designed to take about an hour in a group setting. Adapt it to the time you have available.

Introduction and Chapter 1: Jesus Has a Body

1. What was your experience of reading the introduction and chapter 1 like?

2. What kind of experience did you have with the exercises?

3. Consider what Scripture has to say about the body, using the holy habit of *lectio divina*. This ancient way of spiritual reading invites us to dialogue with God as we encounter Scripture and Scripture encounters us.

    - First, enter into Scripture through the door of silence and solitude. Begin by quieting your heart. Remain in silence for three to five minutes, letting the roar of the day roll away as you rest.

    - *Lectio:* Read the Scripture text aloud the first time, noticing a word or phrase that intrigues or repels.

    - *Meditatio:* Now read the text aloud a second time and spend some time thinking on the text.

    - *Oratio:* For the third reading, quietly dialogue with God about the text and actively respond to him. This may involve jotting something down in your journal or moving to a posture of prayer or praise.

    - *Contemplatio:* Stay quiet and available, open to what God has for you in this psalm. Let solitude be inhabited for a few minutes.

    - As you read the biblical text, let the text also read you. As you question the text, let the text also question you. As you think on the text, also look for ways to be bodily involved with the text, such as responding with hands upraised or by kneeling.

- Share with one another what spoke to you in Psalm 139.

Allow about twenty minutes for this experience.

4. "This is what the LORD says: 'Stand at the crossroads and look; ask for the ancient paths, ask where the good way is, and walk in it, and you will find rest for your souls'" (Jeremiah 6:16 NIV). As you "stand at the crossroads" of beginning this book, what kind of resistance do you notice as you ponder the concept of the physical body as an instrument of holiness for spiritual formation? What intrigues you about this idea?

5. Brainstorm messages about the body that you've encountered this week in the media, at the checkout counter, at work, at church, at home or at the gym. Which messages move you deeper toward holiness of body and integration of body and heart? Which move you further away?

6. The fact is, Jesus has a body just as we do. Discuss how that fact has had an impact on your view of your own body.

7. "Three basic attitudes exist: we are contented and connected to our body as a holy dwelling place of the Living God; we dismiss our body as irrelevant to our walk with God; we revere our body at the expense of our worship of God." Which of these three attitudes are you most drawn to and why?

8. What do you believe about the body's existence beyond our time on earth? How is that perspective affecting your daily treatment of your body? Does that impact how you feel about burial or cremation of the body at death?

9. Hebrews 4:15 says: "For we do not have a high priest who is unable to sympathize with our weaknesses, but we have one [Jesus] who in every respect has been tested as we are, yet without sin." Using the discipline of meditation, reflect on

what that might mean in practical ways for your daily life. For example, where are you being tested right now? How might your relationship with Jesus help you in that test?

Chapter 2: Bodies Within the Body

1. What was your experience of reading chapter 2 like?

2. What kind of experience did you have with the reflection exercises?

3. What is the role of your local place of worship, whether a home church fellowship or a large church group, in addressing issues of the physical body? Do you think this is even a role that Christ-followers should have with one another?

4. What impression does a pastor or ministry leader, overweight, obese or so sadly out of shape that they cannot move with ease, offer to the world and to Christ's followers? What might this say about the interplay of body and soul in relationship to the gospel?

5. What stops us from confronting these blatant, poor lifestyle choices in ourselves? In others? What would help get the conversation going so we can lovingly help one another toward more health and wellness?

6. On an index card, rate your physical, spiritual and mental/emotional health on a scale from 1 to 10, with 1 being poor and 10 being excellent. Brainstorm ways to improve in each of those areas. Choose one thing to improve on in each area of your life.

7. Some people live transparent, authentic lives, letting us know their struggles, yet their struggles are not used as an excuse. Others excuse all their behaviors, blaming family of origin, work stresses or the latest crisis for the disrepair they have allowed themselves to get in. What makes the difference in that choice of attitude and action? Where do you fall in that spectrum?

8. How does Holy Communion influence your view of your body as well as your view of the larger body of Christ? How does what other faith communities teach about the Lord's Supper affect their view of the body?

9. St. Ireneaus said, "The glory of God is a human being fully alive." Celebration and joy are holy habits that make us more fully alive and form us more into the likeness of Christ. When we celebrate, we remember the good and honor the wonder of one another. We rejoice in all that God is and is up to in and for us. Together as a small group, have a party to celebrate one another.

   • Start the party by reading Philippians 4:4, 8 and Hebrews 10:24-25.

   • Take some quiet time to think of the individuals who make up your group and how they are true, noble, right, pure, lovely, admirable, excellent and praiseworthy. Think of ways you can rejoice in who they are and be one another's cheering team.

   • Write three words or phrases on sticky notes that name what you like about your group. For instance, laughter, deep questions and the safety of being together are reasons to rejoice in one another.

   • Place the sticky notes on posterboard, creating a greeting card poster titled "What We Like About Us" that celebrates your group.

   • Read aloud what makes your small group unique, and savor that joy.

   • Reread Hebrews 10:24-25 and Philippians 4:4, 8.

   • Using two index cards, write the name of the person to your right and to your left at the top of each card and one thing you like about each of them. This can be a character trait, like "I like your humble spirit," or a body trait, such as "I like how your eyes sparkle when you laugh."

- Read aloud what was written. (If time allows, other group members can add additional likes to the list.)

- Pray Psalm 133 together aloud as a blessing on one another, recalling how the kind words spoken are a waterfall of joy from God.

Allow twenty to thirty minutes for this celebration of the bodies within your body of Christ.

Chapter 3: Our Body in Worship

1. What was your experience of reading chapter 3 like?

2. What kind of experience did you have with the chapter's reflection exercises?

3. Worship is a holy habit that happens anywhere and at any time. It can occur in the simple moments of life while watching a sunset or laughing among friends or in intentional moments set aside for reflection and praise.

   - Together, enter into a time of worship. Assume a posture of worship that is not your normal worship posture. Notice what feelings arise in your heart toward God in this new manner of expressing love for God.

   - Read Psalm 122:1 aloud.

   - Read Psalm 46:10 aloud. Enter into a time of silence or a time with very quiet music. Light a candle or dim the lights to create an atmosphere of calm solitude. Spend three minutes letting go of the day and becoming present to God and to your own heart. Use all your senses during this time of quiet to engage your body as you worship.

   - Read Psalm 48:9-10 and then Psalm 84 aloud. Using the holy habit of meditation, mull over the words spoken. Spend three minutes marinating in the Word of God and listening for God's voice.

- Spend five minutes speaking aloud what you adore about God: his character, his name and his creation. What worship posture might you try out during this time of praise?

- Read 1 John 1:9 aloud. As you ponder a silent confession to God, move into a different worship posture to express how you feel toward God during confession.

- Read Psalm 141:2 aloud. Spend time praying to God. Is there a new posture you'd like to move into during this prayer time?

- Read Ephesians 5:19-20 aloud, then close your worship by singing a song together.

- Talk about what it was like using your body in new ways to worship.

Allow twenty minutes for this time of worship.

4. How would you explain the holy habit of worship to someone? Would bodily postures be part of that definition?

5. How do you go about choosing a gift for someone you love? In what ways does your worship express your gift of love to God?

6. When you notice other people worshiping God, do any of their body expressions delight you or offend you? Why is this so?

7. What new way might you incorporate your physical body into your daily prayer and Scripture time with God? How could you engage your senses more?

8. Do you find yourself resistant to change? Think of how you respond when someone suggests an activity that you don't really want to do. Think of how you respond to changes in your local faith community. Spend some time as a group reflecting on where that resistance may be coming from.

9. Study the different parts of corporate worship. For example, explore the ancient liturgical forms that are still in use today in many faith communities. How might knowing where these pieces come from affect the way a person worships? How have faith communities in different times and places used the body in worship? For instance, consider the styles of worship among the Egyptian Coptic Church, Latin American Roman Catholic Church, Pentecostal churches in North America or an underground Chinese house church and what role the body plays in each of these worship styles.

Chapter 4: Toward a Balanced Lifestyle

1. What was your experience of reading chapter 4 like?

2. What kind of experience did you have with the chapter's reflection exercises?

3. What role does food play in your life? In Matthew 6:25, Jesus tells his followers not to be anxious about food or drink or clothing because life is more than food and the body more than clothing. How might your emotions impact your attitude toward food and the physical part of daily life?

4. "Preach the gospel at all times and if necessary, use words" is attributed to St. Francis. What might it mean to preach the gospel through your body by the way you use it, the way you care for it, the way you dress it?

5. Write "real food" on the left edge of an index card and "highly processed food" on the right edge. Draw a line between these phrases. As you review your last three meals, place an X on the line indicating where what you ate would fall on the continuum. What is one change you could make to get more foods weighted toward the "real" side of the line?

6. How does your local body of Christ help or hinder healthy eating and exercise habits? What could you choose to do dif-

ferently within that setting to move toward more health and wellness through healthy eating and exercise?

7. First Corinthians 10:31 says: "So, whether you eat or drink, or whatever you do, do everything for the glory of God." Make a list of what exercise you did today. How could you move more this week to bring glory to God in your body?

8. In Ephesians 5:29 we read: "For no one ever hates his own body, but he nourishes and tenderly cares for it, just as Christ does for the church." Yet we all are aware of people, perhaps even ourselves, who hate their body as evidenced by addictions, neglect, cutting, abuse and other poor lifestyle choices, like smoking or misuse of over-the-counter medications. What are the implications for Christ-followers who struggle to love their bodies in the same way Christ cares for and loves the church, his body, here on earth?

9. Paying attention is a large part of growth toward balance in all of life. We notice God; we notice ourselves in response to God. In the Spiritual Exercises of St. Ignatius, the prayer of examen leads to a more examined, intentional life. Through prayerful questions and thoughtful examination, we ask how we have loved God, ourselves and our neighbor in the course of the present day.

   Use this holy habit to notice your own treatment of your body and how that body care engages you more deeply with God or distracts you from engaging with God. With a transition into an awareness of God's love both at the beginning and the end of the prayer, the five steps of the examen allow us to look specifically at our body care across the day and notice the movements of God and our own response, or lack thereof.

   • Be aware of God's love for you as you enter this form of prayer.

- Gratitude notes the gifts from God. What are you thankful for about your body today?

- Petition involves requesting godly insight and strength to honestly examine the day, specifically focused on the body. Ask the Lord to give you clarity and lack of blind spots as you notice your life in your body today.

- Review helps us notice the places where we enter into or resist the invitations and presence of God. Where has God invited you to notice your body and its care? Where have you resisted or missed the invitation?

- Asking forgiveness aligns our heart and unburdens it. What specific moments where you missed God's presence and invitations for body care today will you offer up in confession, for forgiveness?

- Renewal invites us to stand on tiptoe, anticipating tomorrow with a concrete approach as to how to better live attentive to God. Every day is a new beginning. How will you resolve to be more present to your body and God's invitations for the day to come?

- Be aware of God's love for you as you exit this form of prayer, ending your time with praying aloud the Lord's Prayer.

- How did the prayer of examen bring new insight to your interaction with your body and to your relationship with God? What feels comfortable about this type of prayer? What feels awkward?

Allow twenty minutes for the prayer of examen.

Chapter 5: A Theology of Food

1. What was your experience of reading chapter 5 like?

2. What kind of experience did you have with the chapter's reflection exercises?

3. Reread the quote in the chapter from Leslie Leyland Fields:

    > It's potluck Sunday. . . . I have some idea of what the of-
    > ferings will be: hot dogs wrapped in white buns . . . buckets
    > of drive-through fried chicken anchoring the table. Neon-
    > orange cheese doodles will inevitably show up, somewhere
    > near the salads. The greenest item will be several bowls of
    > lime Jell-O with fruit suspended in it, which, I've decided,
    > is to signal its inobvious function as food. We pray our
    > thanks over this smorgasbord of chemical wizardry and
    > marketing genius, ask that it would strengthen our bodies
    > (something I believe will take divine intervention), and
    > invite Jesus to be among us as we eat.[1]

    Do you agree with her assessment, which seems to imply
    that potlucks are questionable places to find food that is healthy
    to eat? Think of potlucks you've attended in the last six months.
    How might the food there affirm or deny her concerns?

4. Do you agree with the chapter's statement "every bite we put in
    our mouth is a political and theological statement"? Why or
    why not? Is there a spiritual discipline listed in appendix A that
    might help you answer this question?

5. Define what the purpose is for food and regular mealtimes with
    family and/or friends. Are there ways you'd like to celebrate the
    positives while resolving to do some things differently?

6. How might you join with others to be part of offering healthy
    food to those in your community? As a holy habit of service
    discerned through the discipline of guidance, pray about where
    and how to become involved in a community outreach in-
    volving food. Could this be something like working in a food
    bank or growing a community garden? Are there areas near
    you where you could offer an outreach to the neighborhood or
    to an area of your region where the access to fresh produce is
    difficult to obtain?

7. Bring one piece of food or its wrapper to small group. Using a world map, trace the journey of these foods from source to table. What do you know about the grower, the harvesters, transportation involved, the grocery store buyers, the costs involved for fuel and pay for workers and other personnel involved in getting that food item from its source to your table? What do you know about more local sources for food?

8. How might your understanding of the Lord's Supper inform the way you approach the issues presented in this chapter?

9. Using the discipline of study, watch fifteen minutes of one of the following secular documentaries or movies, or any other food-themed film. Suggested movies include *Babette's Feast*, *Chocolat* and *Uncle Nino*. Suggested documentaries include *Food, Inc.*, *Fat, Sick & Nearly Dead* and *Forks Over Knives*. Did this change your perspective on food? Will you change anything in your life as a result? (You could also plan a movie night and watch one of these in its entirety together. Then discuss its impact.)

Chapter 6: Questioning Cultural Messages

1. What was your experience of reading chapter 6 like?

2. What kind of experience did you have with the chapter's reflection exercises?

3. Dallas Willard says, "The deepest revelation of our character is what we choose to dwell on in thought, what constantly occupies our mind—as well as what we can or cannot even think of."[2] Philippians 4:8, 2 Corinthians 10:5 and Romans 12:2 point to the importance of our thoughts as they relate to the world in which we live. Examine what kinds of thoughts constantly go through your heart and head. Is there a piece of popular culture that is a part of those thoughts, for good or for ill? Do they speak the truth of the kingdom of God, or do they

speak lies? Decide on ways to use the discipline of submission to control the thoughts of your heart.

4. Because of the incarnation of Jesus, Christianity has allowed depictions of God, Jesus and, in some cases, the host of saints to decorate sacred spaces. What are the advantages and disadvantages of having pictures of Jesus or depictions of God in a worship space instead of abstract art or geometric designs?

5. Some of the pictures mentioned above are called "icons," from the Greek word for images. These are sacred art works, painted under strict guidelines, used regularly by many Christians, especially in Eastern Orthodox churches. Icons are often called "windows into heaven." They are meant not to evoke an emotion but to draw us into the story or scene portrayed. Using books or Internet sites, see examples of icons. What do these teach you about God, yourself and God's work in the world? Some people find icons very helpful in their private prayer times. Others do not connect with them at all. Where are you in the spectrum?

6. How does the pressure of physical appearance and being "in style" impact our understanding of who God is and who we are? Do we believe that God will not love us if we aren't thin enough, pretty enough, smart enough or strong enough? Is there a difference between men and women in this regard? Consider ways to interact with Christ-followers or non-Christ-followers concerning these issues.

7. John 1 talks about "the Word made flesh," referring to Jesus' birth in Bethlehem. How might the Word, Jesus, impact the words we speak, read or write? Is there a difference between Christian literature and books written by Christians? Categorize authors such as Madeleine L'Engle, Flannery O'Connor, Jan Karon, C. S. Lewis and Bret Lott. Using the discipline of study, read short passages from a Christian book and a book

written by a Christian. What struck you about the similarities and the differences between the two?

8.   Create a list of hymns and songs sung in your church or heard on the radio or on an mp3 player over the last few weeks. Examine the lyrics. Are they theologically accurate vehicles that speak truth?

9.   Art gives insight to culture and vice versa. Look at books or Internet sites to see examples of both Michelangelo's *David* and Giacometti's *Three Men Walking,* also known as *Groupe III Hommes II.* If you didn't know anything about either of these sculptures, what would they say to you about the artist's beliefs about humanity, about God and about himself? Now compare these to pictures of women in art over a period of six hundred years and the video at the website maddieruud.hubpages.com/hub/ Standards_of_Beauty_An_Illustrated_Timeline. What stands out to you?

Chapter 7: Extremes Examined

1.   What was your experience of reading chapter 7 like?

2.   What kind of experience did you have with the chapter's reflection exercises?

3.   Reflect on this quote from St. Francis of Assisi:

> Everyone must study his own nature. Some of you can sustain life with less food than others can, and therefore I desire that he who needs more nourishment shall not be obliged to equal others, but that everyone shall give his body what it needs for being an efficient servant of the soul. For as we are obliged to be on our guard against superfluous food which injures body and soul alike, thus we must be on the watch against immoderate fasting, and this the more, because the Lord wants conversion and not victims.[3]

St. Francis encourages a balance that is dictated by what our unique, individual body requires, not by what someone else dictates. The goal is for our body to be an "efficient servant of the soul." Would you describe your body that way? Why or why not?

4. Create a list of mottos or sayings you recall from your childhood that centered on food, as well as a list of who said them, such as parents, relatives, teachers and other leaders. Deduce how these mottos have continually influenced your "theology of eating."[4] How will you disengage from the falsehoods that are part of your past repertoire? With what will you replace those sayings? Think about where you might be influencing young people with similar sayings.

5. A number of authors address issues of healing and freedom. Neil Anderson's *Victory over the Darkness*, John Eldredge's *Waking the Dead* (especially chaps. 6-10), Beth Moore's *Praying God's Word*, Leanne Payne's *The Healing Presence* and Peter Scazzero's *Emotionally Healthy Spirituality* offer ideas on a strong, true self-identity in Christ, prayer, walking with God daily, understanding spiritual warfare, and seeking the guidance and wisdom of Christ-centered professionals, which may lead to emotional and physical freedom from things that entangle exterior and interior places in our life. Where might your body need more prayer and counsel for healing and freedom? What one thing can you do in the next month to begin a deeper journey into freedom?

6. Lent, the forty days before Easter, is traditionally a time of fasting. Many Christ-followers choose a discipline or intentional practice of some kind to focus on during those forty days. What, if any, has been your practice during Lent? How does observing people who are stricter or more lenient than you in their Lenten practice influence you?

7. Jesus touched many "untouchables" in his public ministry of healing; lepers, bleeding women and the dead were all considered "polluted" in Jesus' day. Our English word "salvation" is closely related to the Latin word *salvus*, which means health, wholeness and balance. When Jesus "saved" these people, he did so in body as well as heart. Who is someone that you can bring a healing touch to today? Where do you need to experience Jesus' healing touch?

8. What are your favorite foods? What foods will you not eat, even if served at someone else's house? Do you have food allergies? Would someone describe you as a "picky eater"? Is your distaste of certain foods health based or preference based? If the latter, how did that preference get started?

9. There is much discussion in media today about poor eating choices. There is not as much discussion about the issue of orthorexia, that is, healthy eating taken to an unhealthy extreme. How would you describe your approach to food? Is it healthy? Where might you need to make small changes?

Chapter 8: The Body Gone Awry

1. What was your experience of reading chapter 8 like?

2. What kind of experience did you have with the chapter's reflection exercises?

3. Some common disabilities include hearing loss, poor eyesight or lack of mobility. At times people with these conditions are treated as if their mind is also infirm. Whom do you know who has a common disability? What do you know or want to learn about this condition that might cause you to interact differently with them? Learning about the chronic conditions of your friends and neighbors will enhance your relationship with them while showing them God's grace.

4. A physical therapist noted that there are four kinds of body-

related trauma: physical, emotional, chemical, such as chemotherapy, and nutritional, like that caused by malnutrition. Everyone struggles with some kind of trauma at some point in
life. Some instances last for a short time while others become
long-term, chronic conditions. Think of a time when you suffered trauma. Reflect on how it affected you immediately and
in the long run. How has God touched those places? What still
needs healing?

5. "Gratitude cannot always change circumstances, but it can help
   you see beyond them."[5] Make a list of things you are thankful
   for *in* your current circumstances, though not necessarily *for*
   within your current circumstances. Share your thanksgivings
   with one another.

6. Even for those with a chronic condition, there are still choices
   to be made that can lead either to being as healthy as possible
   within the circumstances or to exacerbating the illness. Brainstorm things that someone you know or even you might be
   able to do.

7. What have you learned from caring for or observing a person
   with a chronic condition? Have you made changes to your own
   lifestyle choices based on what you have learned vicariously
   from them?

8. Jean Vanier founded L'Arche communities, places that care for
   people with physical and mental disabilities (www.larcheusa
   .org). Reflect on these words of Henri J. Nouwen about Day-
   break, a L'Arche community where he lived and ministered:

   > L'Arche, however, is built not on words, but on the body.
   > The community of L'Arche is a community formed around
   > the wounded bodies of handicapped people. Feeding,
   > cleaning, touching, holding—this is what builds the com-
   > munity. Words are secondary. Most handicapped people

have few words to speak, and many do not speak at all. It is the language of body that counts most. "The word became flesh." That is the center of the Christian message. Often the body was seen as a hindrance to the full realization of what the word wanted to express. But Jesus confronts us with the word that can be seen, heard, and touched. The body thus becomes the way to know the word and to enter into relationship with the word. The body of Jesus becomes the way of life.[6]

Consider ways in which you might reach out to those struggling in your community. For instance, is there someone who needs a ride to church or who needs help shopping once a week? Is there someone who needs a short outing periodically? Ask God to show you the person and situation that would fit your gifts and temperament.

9. "Most folks are as happy as they make up their minds to be," said Abraham Lincoln. While chronic illness, debilitating conditions, or everyday illnesses, aches and pains are things we have no control over, we always have control over our attitude by pressing into God. Many emotions arise in difficult situations, perhaps even more so if there is a chronic condition or long-term health issues. Because of the incarnation and the resurrection, the curtain to the Holy of Holies is torn, giving us full access to God anytime. He invites us to come with questions and with emotions such as pain, anger, tiredness, a sense of abandonment and disappointment. The Psalms express the depths of both joys and sorrows. They are a wonderful travel guide on the journey in suffering, in hope for relief and, ultimately, in leading us to reside in the confidence that though God may not change the circumstances, God offers his presence and his comfort always. A number of psalms teach us how to lament as well as how to seek comfort

among the distress of a body gone awry, whether it is our own body or the body of someone we hold dear (see Psalms 13; 23; 31; 35; 41–42; 44; 54–56; 61; 63; 73–74; 79; 86; 88; 91; 102; 105 and 121, among others).

- Enter praying the Psalms with quiet. Put on stillness, becoming aware of God's presence. Put off any distractions that pull you from prayer.

- Read Psalm 13 aloud. Notice what raw emotions arise and stay present to them, not squashing them.

- Slowly reread the psalm silently to yourself. Pray it to God, inserting specifics to the pain and suffering you or someone you love is experiencing.

- Where do you feel forgotten? Where do you feel God's face is hidden from you? Speak these things to God in writing, through a bodily expression or in your heart's dialogue with God.

- What thoughts do you wrestle with? Tell God the questions you have, the things you wonder about surrounding issues of suffering.

- What does your sorrow feel like? How does it manifest itself in emotions, relationships with others and connectedness with God? Be specific as you name these to God.

- When God looks at you, what does he see? How does he answer?

- Where do you feel overwhelmed?

- What foes do you think are being spoken of here, and what is their impact on your heart?

- Are you able to trust God? Be honest with God about your trust and your doubts.

- Do you believe in God's unfailing love for you in this circumstance? Recall where you see and don't see that love currently. Recall times in the past that you've known that unfailing love and what you hope the future will bring.

- What does the song you sing to God say? Is it a song of hope? Of sorrow? Of anger? Of exhaustion?

- Where has God been good to you, even here in this hard place of suffering?

- Together, read Psalm 23 as your closing prayer.

- Share with one another how God met you in praying Psalm 13.

Allow fifteen minutes for praying this psalm.

Chapter 9: Seasoned Well

1. What was your experience of reading chapter 9 like?

2. What kind of experience did you have with the chapter's reflection exercises?

3. What season of life do you think you are in? What challenges and joys are you encountering?

4. What do you wish someone had told you about your body at another season of life to prepare you for the one you are in?

5. Thinking about the people you live with or do life with, how might you offer guidance or mentoring for their season of life? How might they teach you something from their life season?

6. What part of your body's life has moved you to a deeper place with Jesus? Where do you wrestle with the Lord about your body's history, and what are your hopes for your body's future?

7. Holy habits help us hone in on holiness. Which holy habits, spiritual disciplines, have been most significant to you at this season of life? In the last one? Which habits do you anticipate being most significant in the season to come? Think of a new

holy habit you would like to experiment with during this current life season. See appendix A for some suggestions.

8. How much have you thought about and prepared for death? It's a season we must each prepare for as we live. The logistics of funerals are one component to consider. End-of-life choices are vital as well. By creating legal documents, you can specify your requests. What scares you the most about dying?

9. Play and rest are two essential portions to a healthy life, regardless of what season we are in. How much time do you devote to play and rest versus work and worry? How will you weave play and rest into the tapestry of your life this month? Plan something specific and measurable. Tell each other what you are going to do so you can encourage one another with accountability.

Chapter 10: The Next Generation

Whether or not you have children of your own, as the body of Christ we are all to care for the lives of those in a younger generation. Perhaps you are involved with children and youth through church or community activities or by being related to a child or a teenager. Though not all of these questions may directly apply to your situation, consider the flavor of the questions and ponder how you could apply the truth of the questions' theme to your situation.

1. What was your experience of reading chapter 10 like?

2. What kind of experience did you have with the chapter's reflection exercises?

3. Reflecting on what you might be teaching children about food, exercise and their bodies, what changes would you like to see occur within yourself? Within the children in your circle of influence?

4. Is your kitchen the health center of your house? If the members of your small group came to visit, what would they deduce

about your eating habits from looking in your kitchen? What one thing could you change today that could make your kitchen a healthier place for any children in your life?

5. How might you reorient time spent with children toward a more active and outdoorsy lifestyle? In the chapter, Nature Deficit Disorder, a term coined by Richard Louv in his book *Last Child in the Woods*, is mentioned as being associated with a wide range of behavioral problems in children and adults. Brainstorm ways to prevent Nature Deficit Disorder that are specific to your locale.

6. Consider what children eat when they are not at home. What meals and snacks are offered at school, church, birthday parties, fellowship gatherings and sport practices? How might you be a positive influence so that these offerings lead to wise eating habits? For example, could you advocate for healthy school lunches, whether you have school-aged children or not?

7. Aiming toward simplicity, brainstorm ways to create a healthier rhythm in all areas of your life and the lives of any children you may be raising. Are there ways to reduce or eliminate overcommitments, excess busyness, unhealthy foods, long periods of watching TV or surfing the Internet? What wholesome life do you hope to create?

8. A recent newspaper article discussed the question of whether a three-year-old child who is severely overweight at 90 pounds should be taken away from its parents and put in foster care in order to receive proper nutrition and exercise. How would you answer that question? Are you aware of children who are obese or malnourished? Prayerfully consider what your responsibility may be to those children and their families. Is there a family who is struggling that you could partner with, in the spirit of the discipline of service?

9. When children grow up and leave home for college and career, what do you hope they remember about their childhood? What positive beliefs and messages do you hope they recall about their body, their eating habits and exercise?

Chapter 11: Caring for the Planet

1. What was your experience of reading chapter 11 like?

2. What kind of experience did you have with the chapter's reflection exercises?

3. Considering creation leads us to consider God the Creator. Through meditation, solitude, silence and prayer:

   • Ask the Lord to enlighten the eyes of your heart in this time of quiet.

   • Read Matthew 6:25-34.

   • Quietly gaze at a plant, a leaf, a flower arrangement or a rock.

   • What does this natural item tell you of God?

   • What does it tell you of creation?

   • What is it that Jesus hopes we will garner by looking at the flowers of the field or the birds in the air?

   • Read Psalm 104 or Psalm 148 as the closing prayer.

   • Share what pondering creation showed you of the Creator and how that relates to your body and your heart.

   Allow twenty minutes for this experience.

4. Read Wendell Berry's words:

   The ecological teaching of the Bible is simply inescapable: God made the world because He wanted it made. He thinks the world is good, and He loves it. It is His world; He has never relinquished title to it. And He has never revoked the conditions, bearing on His gift to us of the use of it, that oblige us to take excellent care of it. If God loves the world, then how might any person of faith be excused for not loving it or justified in destroying it?[7]

In addition, read Genesis 1:26-31; 2:15-18 and Revelation 21:1-7. What do you notice about creation now and in the future? What is involved in the call to be a good caretaker, stewarding well the earth? Brainstorm things you can do.

5. In baptism, God uses water to claim us as his own. In Holy Communion, we use bread and wine or grape juice. This is a kind of double entendre for the body of Christ: Christ feeds us, his body, the church, with his body and blood. God offers grace through these simple elements of the earth. C. S. Lewis says:

> Here a hand from the hidden country touches not only my soul but my body. . . . Here is a big medicine and strong magic. . . . The command, after all, was Take eat: not Take, understand.[8]

Reflect on why God might use material elements from the earth in the Lord's Supper and baptism. What do you think of Lewis's perspective on these elements?

6. We are aware of one church that uses compostable paper products for its annual Easter breakfast. It is that faith community's attempt to celebrate the resurrection in a way that includes the earth. Would that make a difference in your faith community? Why or why not?

7. What are some simple ways that you can be a little more attentive to caring for the earth this week?

8. Is there a local natural resource or area that you could be a better steward of? How might you pray for that area?

9. Using the discipline of celebration, make a list of your favorite natural places in the country or the world. What makes them

special to you? Thank God for those places as you pray about how you might protect them from damage and exploitation. Psalm 19 says the heavens declare the glory of God. Share a time when you "heard" creation or one of God's creatures praising him.

Conclusion: Going On from Here

1. What was your experience of reading the conclusion like?

2. The body does not matter more than the heart, but it does matter. What happens to the body has an impact on the heart. The question posed in this book is "Is physical health related to spiritual formation?" After reading the book, what is your answer to this question?

3. What do you know about the concept of spiritual direction? Do you know of anyone who has or is a spiritual director? The Evangelical Spiritual Directors Association offers information concerning this ministry of discernment and companionship in prayer. Consider exploring this type of spiritual relationship as one manner of moving deeper with God as you integrate your body with your heart. You can find more information about spiritual direction and a list of spiritual directors at www .ecswisdom.org/index.php/esda.

4. Pick three things you learned in this book that you want to explore further and/or incorporate into your life. What specific, measurable plan will you enlist to help you? Who will partner with you for accountability?

5. What topics do you wish this book had addressed about the body? What topic surprised you the most as you read about it?

6. Develop a rule of life.

    *   Start simply; prayerfully develop some overarching principles that you will live by, using the discipline of submission.

- Consider having a principle for your body, for your spiritual life, for your work life and for the relationships in your life. For example, a rule might look like this:

  a. My body is an important part of who I am. Therefore, I will exercise for thirty minutes four times each week. One of those times will be an outside activity with my family.

  b. I believe a rhythm of rest and refreshment is as important as good, honest work. Therefore, I will leave work every day at 6 p.m.

  c. I believe that my relationship with God informs all aspects of my life. Therefore, I will take a prayer walk during lunch once a week.

- Focus on overarching principles that work themselves out into specific and measurable steps. If the rule is too rigid, it will be more likely to fail. Your rule will change as your season of life changes. Things you cannot do now may be possible in another season of life.

- Use your rule of life as a guide for discernment when asked to take on a new challenge at work or join a committee at church.

- Share your rule with a close friend.

- Ask them to help hold you accountable.

4. As you close your time in this book, thank God for your body by praying through 1 Corinthians 3:16.

Notes

Introduction

[1]Final student paper from MSFL course.

[2]See 2 Corinthians 5:10: "For all of us must appear before the judgment seat of Christ, so that each may receive recompense for what has been done in the body, whether good or evil."

Chapter 2: Bodies Within the Body

[1]Dietrich Bonhoeffer, *Life Together* (New York: Harper & Row, 1954), p. 30.

[2]Ibid., p. 89.

Chapter 3: Our Body in Worship

[1]G. P. Mellick Belshaw, ed., *Lent with Evelyn Underhill* (Harrisburg, PA: Morehouse, 1990), p. 62.

[2]Frederick Buechner, *Wishful Thinking: A Seeker's ABC* (New York: HarperSanFrancisco, 1973, 1993), p. 122.

Chapter 4: Toward a Balanced Lifestyle

[1]See http://thinkexist.com/quotes/Steven_R._Covey.

[2]See http://diabetes.webmd.com/features/reversing-type-2-diabetes. Also see the book by Jack Challem and Ron Hunninghake, M. D., *Stop Prediabetes Now: The Ultimate Plan to Lose Weight and Prevent Diabetes* (Hoboken, NJ: Wiley, 2009).

[3]While technically processed foods include a banana or potato that have been peeled or fresh-picked vegetables that have been canned or frozen, the term "highly processed food" has come to indicate something we eat that is far from its natural state and, therefore, less nutritious. Generally these foods are high in sodium, refined sugars and saturated fats, and provide what is known as "empty calories." Diets high in these substances are linked directly to diseases such as colorectal, kidney and stomach cancers. The following

website goes in greater depth about this: http://health.amuchbetterway.com/
how-do-you-define-processed-food/.

[4]See www.gettheworldmoving.com/the-science/employees.

[5]See www.gettheworldmoving.com/about-us/research/lancaster-university-study.

[6]See http://jap.physiology.org/content/98/1/3.short.

[7]Michael Pollan uses these terms in his writing and speaking.

Chapter 5: A Theology of Food

[1]Sustainable agriculture is a way of raising food that is healthy for consumers
and animals, does not harm the environment, is humane for workers, re-
spects animals, provides a fair wage to the farmer, and supports and en-
hances rural communities. See www.sustainabletable.org/intro/whatis.

[2]Michael Pollan, in his speaking and writing, makes the distinction between
edible food-like substances and real food. See chapter four for more discussion of this concept.

[3]This is an example of what one church is doing to help feed those who are
nutritionally challenged. See www.theamia.org/new/features/faith-in-action/
food4all-at-old-north-abbey.

[4]Benjamin M. Stewart, *A Watered Garden: Christian Worship and Earth's
Ecology* (Minneapolis: Augsburg Fortress, 2001), p. 73.

[5]For example, Dr. Harash Narang writes for the Institute of Science in Society:

> Many chemicals taken in by the body cannot be excreted.
> Therefore, their concentration will increase over time. Such a build
> up of insecticide and herbicide residues in our bodies may be enough
> to produce cancerous effects. There is also evidence to suggest that
> such chemicals are excreted in mother's milk, which will not be good
> for baby.
>
> Herbicide residues in food are already a serious issue. Herbicide-
> tolerant GM crops are engineered to be tolerant to broad-spectrum her-
> bicides which kill all other species of plants indiscriminately. Insects,
> birds and mammals, which depend on those plants, will also die out.
> These herbicides will have drastic effects on biodiversity.
>
> GM companies engineer crops to be tolerant to their own herbicide.
> Studies on glufosinate, one such herbicide, shows that when ingested
> by pregnant females it causes birth defects and defeats in behaviour and
> learning in offspring. Furthermore, fathers exposed to glufosinate also
> gave birth to children with birth defects while exposure to most other
> pesticides did not cause such effects. Glyphosate, another broad-
> spectrum herbicide contained in a formulation commonly known as
> Roundup Ready, has been linked to non-Hodgkin's lymphoma. Claims
> by officials that the herbicides used with GM crops have no harmful
> side effects are false.

See http://ratical.org/co-globalize/MaeWanHo/bse.html#p5.

[6]See www.montereybayaquarium.org/cr/cr_seafoodwatch/sfw_recommenda tions.aspx?c=ln.

[7]Lisa Turner, "Soft(er) Drinks," *Better Nutrition*, August 2011, p. 44-45. This article briefly outlines the long-term consequences of drinking soda pop. Natural sodas, while containing fewer to no chemicals, still contain large quantities of sugars. They are not necessarily a wholesale substitution for traditional brands.

[8]Leslie Leyland Fields, "A Feast Fit for the King," *Christianity Today*, November 2010, pp. 22-28.

[9]Stewart, *A Watered Garden*, pp. 62-63.

[10]Nicholas Bakalar, "Behavior: Distracted Eating Adds More to Waistlines," *The New York Times*, January 3, 2011, www.nytimes.com/2011/01/04/health/research/04behavior.html?_r=1, speaks to this issue.

[11]Percy Dearmer, "Draw Us in the Spirit's Tether," in Evangelical Lutheran Church in America, *Evangelical Lutheran Worship* (Minneapolis: Augsburg Fortress, 2006), hymn 470.

Chapter 6: Questioning Cultural Messages

[1]Generally speaking, the U.S. Department of Agriculture recommends men get between 2,000 and 3,000 calories per day and women should take in 1,600 to 2,400 calories each day. The variance is related to how active a person is, as well as such factors as bone size and age.

[2]See http://lubbockonline.com/news/042597/paradise.htm.

[3]Note: "true" does not necessarily equal nonfiction. There is much in fictionalized art that portrays aspects of God and humanity with honesty and integrity even as it comes in a setting that is not historical.

[4]Movement teaches our muscles subconsciously. There are fields of study that deal with "muscle memory" as part of healing the body and the mind/soul. See http://drjking.wrytestuff.com/swa439224.htm, http://healing.about.com/od/exercise/a/intent_relax.htm and http://healingexperiences.blogspot.com/2010/01/muscle-memory-and-trigger-point-therapy.html for a few places where these issues are discussed.

Chapter 7: Extremes Examined

[1]Peter Kreeft, *Back to Virtue* (San Francisco: Ignatius Press, 1992), p. 181.

[2]Personal email with Lane Arnold, February 25, 2012.

[3]Personal conversation with Lane Arnold, March 2012.

[4]Ibid.

[5]See http://life.gaiam.com/article/when-eating-good-bad for more on orthorexia.

[6]Personal correspondence with Valerie Hess, March 2012. See www.health-science.com/microwave_hazards.html for why some people believe microwaving food is bad for your health.

[7]The Celtic church in Ireland was an exception to this. They kept a sense of the goodness of the material world and viewed it as another witness to God's love and mercy.

[8]Another example is the Hermanos Penitentes, found today in parts of New Mexico and southern Colorado. They are a secret society, who, to atone for their sins, practice penances which consist principally of flagellation, carrying heavy crosses and binding one's body to a cross by tying the limbs to hinder the circulation of blood. There are many versions of this kind of extreme devotional piety throughout the world. Another example is the pilgrimage route to the Cathedral of Santiago de Compostela in Spain, one of the more well-known areas where some pilgrims crawl for miles on their knees as an act of penitence.

[9]George E. Gringras, translator and annotator, *Egeria: Diary of a Pilgrimage*, Ancient Christian Writers (New York: Newman Press, 1970), pp. 230-31.

[10]Fr. Richard Rohr, adapted from *Eucharist as Touchstone* CD and shared in his daily e-mail meditation from the Center for Action and Contemplation, March 25, 2011. See www.cacradicalgrace.org.

Chapter 8: The Body Gone Awry
[1]Personal conversation with Lane Arnold, March 2012.

Chapter 9: Seasoned Well
[1]See www.cbsnews.com/8301-505146_162-57355028/how-old-are-you-really. Also see www.realage.com, where you can figure out your own chronological age.

Chapter 10: The Next Generation
[1]For more discussion on this idea, see Valerie E. Hess and Marti Watson Garlett, *Habits of a Child's Heart: Raising Your Kids with the Spiritual Disciplines* (Colorado Springs: NavPress, 2004).

[2]See www.quotationspage.com/quote/27576.html.

[3]See www.foodrenegade.com/lessons-on-real-food-from-100-years-ago, a blog about the history of "imitation" foods in the US. Michael Pollan also comments on "edible" vs. "food." For further commentary from him on how to eat well, see www.webmd.com/food-recipes/news/20090323/7-rules-for-eating.

[4]The website www.cmbm.org/category/food-as-medicine is one place to begin learning more about this concept.

[5]See www.mayoclinic.com/health/healthy-diet/NU00200. This Mayo Clinic site lists nutrition guidelines for fats, sugar, salt and other nutritional components.

[6]King Arthur Flour Company (which neither of us is associated with in any way) sells a white whole-wheat flour made from white wheat instead of red wheat. It is milder in flavor and can be substituted in many foods for white flour or used half and half with white flour. It is a whole grain but very light; your kids may not even notice the switch. You can find it at the King Arthur Flour Company website, www.kingarthurflour.com, or in many grocery stores.

[7]For more healthy food ideas with children visit www.webmd.com/parenting/healthy-eating-helping-your-child-learn-healthy-eating-habits.

[8]See http://nutrition.wsu.edu/ebet/background.html.

[9]"You're Invited to Dinner with Dr. Oz," *O Magazine,* September 2011, p. 226. Terri Trespicio also writes, "A meal shared with family and friends sustains you in more ways than one," in "Ten Thoughts on Whole Living," *Whole Living,* November 2011, p. 91.

[10]Richard Louv, *Last Child in the Woods: Saving Our Children from Nature-Deficit Disorder* (Chapel Hill, NC: Algonquin Books of Chapel Hill, 2005).

[11]Valerie E. Hess and Marti Watson Garlett, *Habits of a Child's Heart: Raising Your Kids with the Spiritual Disciplines* (Colorado Springs: NavPress, 2004). Pages 49-64 list concrete ways one might teach this discipline well to children of specific ages.

Chapter 11: Caring for the Planet

[1]See www.st-francis-medal.com/st-francis-blessing-of-the-animals.htm.

[2]See www.guidetopsychology.com/gubbio.htm.

[3]Available online at www.washingtoninst.org/1130/19-iii-for-stewardship-of-creation.

[4]Pantheism is the worship of nature; it says God is the material world. Panentheism says all is in God, a concept supported by Colossians 1:17.

[5]Nahum M. Sarna, *The JPS Torah Commentary* (Philadelphia: Jewish Publication Society, 1989), p. 12. The commentary goes on to say that the reason the human race cannot exploit nature is because it is not inherently sovereign. Humanity enjoys its dominion solely by the grace of God. Also, the word used here refers to a monarch's power. In Israel, the monarch did not possess unrestrained power and authority but was limited in his rule by carefully defined and circumscribed divine law. Humanity's subduing of the earth is as a steward who must give an account to God.

[6]John Stott, *The Birds, Our Teachers: Biblical Lessons from a Lifelong Bird-Watcher* (Peabody, MA: Hendrickson, 2000/2007), pp. 94-95. In his footnote on page 96, Stott further writes: "The tragic disappearance of 'the birds of the air' as a result of divine judgment is a regular theme of the prophets. See Jeremiah 9:10 and 12:4, Hosea 4:3, and Zephaniah 1:3."

Conclusion

[1]Stephen A. Macchia, *Crafting a Rule of Life: An Invitation to the Well-Ordered Way* (Downers Grove, IL: InterVarsity Press, 2012), p. 14.

[2]Lane M. Arnold, on my blog, lanearnold.com.

[3]Ibid.

[4]Personal email to Lane Arnold, March 8, 2012.

Appendix A: Holy Habits for the Whole Body

[1]Trevor Hudson, *Discovering Our Spiritual Identity: Practices for God's Beloved* (Downers Grove, IL: InterVarsity Press, 2010), p. 186, emphasis added. Following this quote, Hudson offers guidelines we might use to begin to incorporate the spiritual disciplines in intentional ways into our daily life. The

materials from Renovaré (www.renovare.org) offer the same guidance.

[2]Dennis W. Bakke, *Joy at Work: A Revolutionary Approach to Fun on the Job* (Hollywood, CA: PVG, 2006), p. 134.

Appendix D: Small Group Guide

[1]Leslie Leyland Fields, "A Feast Fit for the King," *Christianity Today*, November 2010, pp. 22-28.

[2]Dallas Willard, *The Divine Conspiracy: Rediscovering Our Hidden Life in God* (New York: HarperOne, 1998), p. 324.

[3]See http://dailychristianquote.com/dcqassisi.html.

[4]Wirzba uses this same term, "theology of food." See Norman Wirzba, *Food and Faith: A Theology of Eating* (New York: Cambridge University Press, 2011).

[5]Terri Trespicio, "Ten Thoughts on Whole Living," *Whole Living*, November 2011, p. 91.

[6]Quoted in Susan A. Blain, ed., *Imaging the Word: An Arts and Lectionary Resource, Volume 2* (Cleveland: United Church Press, 1995), p. 262.

[7]Wendell Berry, *What Are People For?* (New York: North Point Press, 1990), p. 98.

[8]C. S. Lewis, *Letters to Malcolm: Chiefly on Prayer* (New York: Mariner Books, 2002), pp. 103-4.

formatio

TRADITION. EXPERIENCE.
TRANSFORMATION.

Formatio books from InterVarsity Press follow the rich tradition of the church in the journey of spiritual formation. These books are not merely about being informed, but about being transformed by Christ and conformed to his image. Formatio stands in InterVarsity Press's evangelical publishing tradition by integrating God's Word with spiritual practice and by prompting readers to move from inward change to outward witness. InterVarsity Press uses the chambered nautilus for Formatio, a symbol of spiritual formation because of its continual spiral journey outward as it moves from its center. We believe that each of us is made with a deep desire to be in God's presence. Formatio books help us to fulfill our deepest desires and to become our true selves in light of God's grace.

What is Renovaré?

Renovaré USA is a nonprofit Christian organization that models, resources, and advocates fullness of life with God experienced, by grace, through the spiritual practices of Jesus and of the historical Church. We imagine a world in which people's lives flourish as they increasingly become like Jesus.

Through personal relationships, conferences and retreats, written and web-based resources, church consultations, and other means, Renovaré USA pursues these core ideas:

- *Life with God* - The aim of God in history is the creation of an all-inclusive community of loving persons with God himself at the center of this community as its prime Sustainer and most glorious Inhabitant.

- *The Availability of God's Kingdom* - Salvation is life in the kingdom of God through Jesus Christ. We can experience genuine, substantive life in this kingdom, beginning now and continuing through all eternity.

- *The Necessity of Grace* - We are utterly dependent upon Jesus Christ, our ever-living Savior, Teacher, Lord, and Friend for genuine spiritual transformation.

- *The Means of Grace* - Amongst the variety of ways God has given for us to be open to his transforming grace, we recognize the crucial importance of intentional spiritual practices and disciplines (such as prayer, service, or fasting).

- *A Balanced Vision of Life in Christ* - We seek to embrace the abundant life of Jesus in all its fullness: contemplative, holiness, charismatic, social justice, evangelical, and incarnational.

- *A Practical Strategy for Spiritual Formation* - Spiritual friendship is an essential part of our growth in Christlikeness. We encourage the creation of Spiritual Formation Groups as a solid foundation for mutual support and nurture.

- *The Centrality of Scripture* - We immerse ourselves in the Bible: it is the great revelation of God's purposes in history, a sure guide for growth into Christlikeness, and an ever rich resource for our spiritual formation.

- *The Value of the Christian Tradition* - We are engaged in the historical "Great Conversation" on spiritual formation developed from Scripture by the Church's classical spiritual writings.

Christian in commitment, ecumenical in breadth, and international in scope, Renovaré USA helps us in becoming like Jesus. The Renovaré Covenant succinctly communicates our hope for all those who look to him for life:

> In utter dependence upon Jesus Christ as my ever-living
> Savior, Teacher, Lord, and Friend,
> I will seek continual renewal through:
> • spiritual exercises • spiritual gifts • acts of service

RENOVARÉ

Renovaré USA
8 Inverness Drive East, Suite 102 • Englewood, CO, 80112 USA • 303-792-0152
www.renovare.us